# WRITTEN FOR OUR LEARNING

## MAPPING THE OLD TESTAMENT FOR KIDS

Karen Puckett

KAIO PUBLICATIONS, INC.

*Written For Our Learning*
Copyright © 2019 by Karen Puckett
Published by Kaio Publications

All rights reserved. No part of this publication may be reproduced, stored in a retrieval system, or transmitted in any form by any means, electronic, mechanical, photocopy, recording, or otherwise, without the prior permission of the author, except as provided for by USA copyright law.

First printing 2019
Printed in the United States of America

Scripture taken from the New King James Version, unless otherwise indicated.
Copyright © 1982 by Thomas Nelson, Inc. Used by permission. All rights reserved.
ISBN: 978-1-7326661-1-5

Cover design & interior layout by Ben Giselbach

# TABLE OF CONTENTS

About this Book ..................................................................................................................... iii

Lesson 1: God's Covenant with Abraham: No Laughing Matter .......................................... 9

Lesson 2: Isaac and Rebekah: A Marriage Made in Heaven ............................................... 13

Lesson 3: Jacob and Esau: Fighting and Forgiving Brothers .............................................. 17

Lesson 4: Joseph: Serving God in Affliction ...................................................................... 21

Lesson 5: Joseph: Blessings Through God's Providence .................................................... 27

Lesson 6: Moses: Excuses, Excuses, Excuses! ................................................................... 33

Lesson 7: Aaron: A Golden Mistake by Following the Herd ............................................. 39

Lesson 8: Rahab: Salvation When the Walls Come Tumbling Down ................................ 43

Lesson 9: Ehud: King Eglon Gets the Point ....................................................................... 49

Lesson 10: Samson: A Bad Hair Day ................................................................................. 53

Lesson 11: Job: Joy Through Suffering .............................................................................. 57

Lesson 12: Hannah: Teaching by Example ........................................................................ 61

Lesson 13: Saul: Handsome Leader with an Ugly Heart .................................................... 65

Lesson 14: Uzzah: Good Intentions Without Obedience Does not Please God ................. 71

Lesson 15: Solomon: Wisdom for the Ages ....................................................................... 75

Lesson 16: Rehoboam and Jeroboam: God Divides the Nation ......................................... 81

Lesson 17: Elijah: With God on His Side, It's no Contest ................................................. 85

Lesson 18: Naaman: A Child Shall Lead Him ................................................................... 89

Lesson 19: Athaliah and Joash: The Infant King Grandma Forgot .................................... 93

Lesson 20: Jonah and Nahum: The Rest of the Story ........................................................ 97

Lesson 21: Hezekiah: Faith Strong Enough to Turn Back Time ...................................... 103

Lesson 22: Josiah: Taking God's Word Seriously ........................................................... 109

Lesson 23: Shadrach, Meshach, and Abednego: On Fire for the Lord ............................. 113

Lesson 24: Ezra and Nehemiah: The Remnant Returns and Rebuilds .............................. 117

Lesson 25: Esther: The Right Place at the Right Time .................................................... 123

Lesson 26: Malachi: The Last Word Before *The Word* ................................................ 127

Supplemental Material ...................................................................................................... 131

# ABOUT THIS BOOK

*Written for Our Learning* is a comprehensive Bible class curriculum contained in one book that provides an effective, fresh approach to teaching students in grades 1–8.

## WHAT MAKES THIS CURRICULUM DIFFERENT?

1. Instead of simply re-telling certain events of the Old Testament, the guide takes it a step further: illustrating how God's plan of salvation has its roots in God's covenant with Abraham.
2. The selected events (the more fictional-sounding word *stories* is not used in the guide) not only paint a vivid historical picture of fascinating Old Testament characters but more importantly, show the endurance of God's covenant in spite of the Israelites' repeated betrayal of Him.
3. The guide is also an introduction to the Old Testament as a whole, designed to give students a clear understanding of the order of major events during the 1,500 years between God's covenant with Abraham through Malachi's final words to the Israelites a little over 400 years before the birth of Christ. Students learn where familiar people and events fit in chronologically in the Old Testament.
4. Many lessons feature Old Testament people and events that preteens may not be as familiar with, giving them the opportunity to expand their knowledge and discovering "the rest of the story." (For example, they probably remember God spares the people of Ninevah at the end of Jonah, but do they know what happens to them later in Nahum?)
5. With a strong emphasis on the Word, each lesson is rich in Scripture, not only the verses from the day's lesson, but also activities that encourage students to search verses elsewhere in the Bible. Some activities offer opportunities for higher-level students to learn how to use Bible concordances and other aids.

## WHAT MAKES THIS TEACHING APPROACH DIFFERENT?

1. The guide is designed to serve eight grade levels efficiently and effectively in one book, eliminating the need to purchase multiple books. In addition, there are no accompanying workbooks as the guide provides all of the information the teacher needs to prepare solid, Bible-based lessons.
2. The format allows both the first-grade teacher and the eighth-grade teacher to cover the same lessons from the same book on the same day, using the "Scribe" or the "Scholar" activities designed specifically for their age groups.
3. For those in charge of education programs wanting to avoid subject-repetition year after year, the guide is a good way to ensure their teachers are on the same page. Literally
4. For those in charge of teaching the preteens, the guide provides thorough background and Scripture references to aid in their lesson preparation. In addition, the teacher has many choices in

terms of activities to support the lesson that he/she can present fresh material each week to keep their students engaged in class participation.

In both its design concept and its teaching approach, *Written for Our Learning* meets not only the needs of the teachers and education program leaders, but also, most importantly, the young impressionable recipients of these Biblical lessons that will help shape their lives in the future.

The 26 lessons in *Written for Our Learning* are written to enable the teacher to reach three overall goals each week:

1. To show the enduring prevalence and relevance of God's covenant with Abraham, eventually leading to His plan of salvation in the New Testament, through the lives of the Israelites, emphasizing that God always keeps His promises (Genesis 17:5-7).
2. To make a practical application in terms appropriate for the age level, illustrating that lessons learned thousands of years ago are still useful today (Rom. 15:4).
3. To present the Biblical text in a manner that not only enriches and expands the students' knowledge of the Old Testament, but also encourages a love for God's Word (Psalm 119:47-48).

## WHAT ARE THE SCRIBE AND SCHOLAR LEVELS?

In order to achieve these goals, each lesson contains many activities that support the Biblical text and encourage class participation. The teacher can plainly see which activity is appropriate for his/her grade level as each activity is clearly coded as **SCRIBE** Level (generally intended for 1–4 grades) or **SCHOLAR** Level (5–8 grades). Some activities are designed for both levels. The teacher uses his/her discretion to choose the activities and the levels best suit the students. Although each lesson covers two class periods (typically Sunday morning and Wednesday night), the guide provides more activities than can be completed during that time. This allows the teacher to have extra options to consider when customizing the best lesson for his/her students.

The **BIBLE WORD OF THE DAY** and **BIBLE BASICS** sections are designed for both **SCHOLAR** and **SCRIBE** levels.

Note: The lesson text, the summary of the Biblical account of the event with embedded Scriptures, is always intended for both Scribe and Scholar levels as it is written. However, a teacher who wants to extract any or all of the read-aloud verses should paraphrase the verses to fill in the gaps.

## CAN YOU GIVE A BREAKDOWN OF EACH LESSON'S ACTIVITIES?

Designed to help teachers in their preparation and their presentation of each lesson, *Written for Our Learning* is unique because of the wide range of activities that promote an atmosphere in which the students come to class eager to learn. Because each lesson is intended to be taught in one week (typically Sunday morning and Wednesday night classes), the activities offered in each lesson cannot be adequately covered in that time frame. This allows the teacher to customize or select the activities to fit the students' needs. By choosing different activities every week or so, the classroom routine never becomes routine. Following are explanations of the lesson outline and different activities found in each lesson. See the next section, Continuous **BESIDE THE POINT** Activities for ongoing projects and games as additional learning tools.

Note: Depending on the nature of the text that week, some lessons may include two separate activities, each for the **SCRIBE** or **SCHOLAR** levels, for a particular section. Others may include only one level of an activity in a section.

##  BEFORE THE EVENT:

This is a brief synopsis of the events that occurred between last week's lesson and this week's lesson but not covered at any length in class. The purpose is to provide the teacher with background information to gain a better understanding of the overall timeline of events as he prepares the upcoming lesson. While it's intended for the teacher's benefit, the teacher may choose to incorporate any or all of the background into the lesson if he determines it benefits his students, too.

## BIBLE VERSES TO BE READ ALOUD:

These are selected verses embedded as part of the lesson's summary text to be read aloud by students or the teacher. The teacher is encouraged to read (or have students read) at least one or two verses along with re-telling the event. This reminds the students that the event you're presenting to them comes directly from the Bible and actually happened.

##  BIBLE WORD OF THE DAY:

The purpose of **BIBLE WORD OF THE DAY** is for the students to build their Bible vocabulary. The **BIBLE WORD OF THE DAY** includes the passage where it's found in that week's Scripture text and in other verses elsewhere in the Bible. It also gives a short, simple definition according to how it's used in the verses.

The word selected in each lesson's **BIBLE WORD OF THE DAY** section generally falls in one or two categories: 1) They are everyday words with a definition common to most preteen students but also have lesser-known, different meanings in the Bible. An example is *seed*, which means descendant (Genesis 21:12). 2) The other category includes words the students probably have heard often in sermons or classes but may not know their meanings. An example is *blameless*, meaning one who cannot be accused of wrongdoing before God or man. Abraham was described as blameless (Genesis 17:1). Students who build their vocabulary at a young age have a head start on building their knowledge of God's Word throughout their lifetime.

##  BIG IDEA:

This one sentence reflects the lesson's the main point or practical application. Some lessons feature more than one **BIG IDEA**, each appropriate for the **SCRIBE** and **SCHOLAR** levels. The teacher's goal is to make sure the students really "get" the **BIG IDEA**.

##  BIBLE BASICS:

These questions focus on the facts of the lesson: the who, what, when, where, and how type of questions that test the students' basic recall of the text. Questions from previous lessons serve as a handy review of the material covered up to that point and are presented for both **SCRIBE** and **SCHOLAR** levels.

## BRING IT UP:

**BRING IT UP** questions, unlike those in the **BIBLE BASICS** section, ask "Why?" The purpose is to motivate these young creative thinkers to put themselves in Old Testament person's shoes or consider their own actions in situations related to the day's lesson. The teacher who carefully guides such as discussion helps them to apply the

Big Idea in their own lives.

##  BESIDE THE POINT:

This activity generally supports the **BIG IDEA** or another important aspect of the lesson with an emphasis on making a practical application. However, in some lessons, the **BESIDE THE POINT** section focuses on another event related to the main event that week. The activities vary from having the students research their own genealogical charts to creating a news report on an Old Testament event.

## → BEYOND THE LESSON:

Students look up Scriptures to find the answer to a question that connects the day's lesson with another event, person, etc. found elsewhere in the Bible. It's conducive for students to solve individually or collectively. Example: Read 2 Kings 4:42-44 and Matthew 14:13-21. What do these two events have in common and how are they different? Answer: Elisha feeds 100 men with 20 loaves of bread. Jesus feeds 5,000 men with five loaves of bread and two fishes.

##  BRING IT HOME:

This activity occurs outside of the classroom and inside the students' homes. So, it's actually homework. A simple lesson, question, or Bible verse is provided for the students to talk about with their parents. It's a good way to keep the parents in the loop concerning Bible class topics and to keep them personally involved in their Bible class studies.

## ADDITIONAL ACTIVITIES:

To supplement the activities that focus on specific points and events from each lesson, the following are suggestions for ongoing projects and occasional games that increase the students' general knowledge of the Old Testament as a whole.

### 1. Flashcards

There are two sets of flash cards included in the guide: 39 Old Testament books and 39 Old Testament people. One side of each card contains the O.T. book or O.T. character, and the flip side of each contains a description of that book or character. Because of their simplicity, these flashcards are excellent teaching tools using repetitive, interactive games. They come in handy to use with students who come early to class or to use to fill a few minutes at the end of class. Or, they are perfect for an indoor game of Four-Square, where, instead of serving a bouncy ball to the opponent, the server sends a flash card to the opponent, who then must give the correct answer found on the other side of the card. If the student answers incorrectly, the next student returns the serve. To help the students learn the Old Testament books in order, the teacher deals all 39 cards to each student. Each student knows only the cards he or she is holding. In a fun game teaching them the importance of teamwork, the students work together to put all of the cards in correct order within a certain time limit. For **SCRIBE** and **SCHOLAR** levels.

### 2. Timeline

Armed with a box of crayons, the **SCRIBE** level students are likely to maintain an active interest in this ongoing and creative project although the **SCHOLARS** may enjoy it, too. They will take pride in showcasing their artistic talents and, whether they realize it or not, will recall what they learned in class because they created visual remind-

# WRITTEN FOR OUR LEARNING

ers of the lessons.

Using the two timelines included in the guide, the teacher finds this to be an easy project to maintain throughout the semester. All that's needed is probably already in the classroom—crayons, colored pencils, markers, etc.—and a large roll of white paper. The teacher simply unrolls the paper as the students create their chronological masterpieces and rolls up the paper and stores it in a corner until the next time the students work on it.

Why keep all the Old Testament knowledge and artistic talents hidden from the rest of the congregation? One suggestion is to invite some people from the congregation who would appreciate a view of the final product: parents, grandparents, older members of the church, church secretary, etc. will enjoy dropping by during the last few minutes of class so the students can give them a visual and audio tour of their timeline, presenting their art and explaining the significance of the Biblical events.

## 3. The Old Testament Scribes

Appropriate for the **SCHOLAR** level, the Old Testament Scribes is a group of writers from the class who enjoy keeping a diary or a journal. In this case, they keep a record of things they hear and read outside of Bible class that relate to the Old Testament. They may jot down a verse from the Old Testament they heard in a sermon or another read during the family devotional. Perhaps they come across a show on The History Channel, for example, about the search for Noah's Ark. Or they hear an adult describe a friend as having "the patience of Job." By being alert, they will be surprised to learn how often the Old Testament in some form comes into play in day-to-day life more than 2,000 years later. The teacher should allow the Old Testament Scribes to report on their Old Testament findings from time to time in class.

## 4. Concordance Challenge

Also a **SCHOLAR** activity, Concordance Challenge is basically an extension of the **BIBLE WORD OF THE DAY**. The purpose is to introduce and teach upper level students to use a Bible concordance through researching the **BIBLE WORD OF THE DAY**. By looking up the **BIBLE WORD OF THE DAY** in their concordances, they discover a list of other Scriptures containing that same word. The Challenge has a two-fold purpose: 1) To give students practice in finding specific verses throughout the entire Bible, and 2) To provide a better understanding of the meaning of the **BIBLE WORD OF THE DAY** by reading these verses.

**WRITTEN FOR OUR LEARNING**

## - LESSON 1 -

# GOD'S COVENANT WITH ABRAHAM: NO LAUGHING MATTER

Scripture Text: Genesis 12:1-9, 17; 18:1-15

 ## BEFORE THE EVENT:

Interestingly, about half of the entire Old Testament period—or 2,000 years—is recorded in just the first 11 chapters of Genesis. Ten chapters focus on Adam and his family, and then on Noah and his family and the Ark.

- Creation (Genesis 1–2): God creates the heavens and the earth, animals and man in six days, resting on the seventh.
- Fall of Man (Genesis 3): Because Adam and Eve eat from the specifically forbidden Tree of the Knowledge of Good and Evil, sin enters the world (vs. 6).
- First Murder (Genesis 4): First son Cain kills his brother Abel because of jealousy involving their sacrifices to God.
- Adam's Family (Genesis 5): Adam has another son, Seth, after Abel dies. Seth's descendant is Enoch, who "walked with God" and was the father of Methuselah, who is recorded in the Bible as the longest-living man at 969 years (vs. 21-24). Enoch and later the prophet Elijah (2 Kings 2:11) are the only two people who do not die but are taken from earth by God.
- Noah's Ark (Genesis 6–8): God is grieved over man's wickedness and evil heart and decides to destroy man from the face of the earth. Noah, because he found favor with God, is spared along with his family.
- God's Covenant with Noah (Genesis 9:8-17): God promises Noah and his descendants that He will never to destroy earth with a flood, using a rainbow as the symbol to remind them of His covenant.

 ## LESSON:

Think about a book you really enjoyed reading. Or maybe it's a book your teacher or parent read to you. Did it have interesting characters or a fascinating story that kept you turning the page? Was it well written or have a central theme? It's hard to put down a book like that!

What better book has all these features and much more than the best-

 ## BIBLE WORD OF THE DAY:

BLAMELESS

Definition: Cannot be accused of wrongdoing before man or God (Genesis 17:1).

*"You shall be **blameless** before the Lord your God"* (Deuteronomy 18:13).

## BIBLE VERSES

Genesis 12:1-3
Genesis 17:7-8
Genesis 18:12
Genesis 21:6-7

 ## BIG IDEA

**(SCHOLAR)** God's plan of salvation that we read about in the New Testament has its roots in the Old Testament.

**(SCRIBE)** Studying the Old Testament gives us a better understanding of the New Testament.

selling book of all time? The Bible! More than five billion copies of this captivating book have been sold worldwide. It's no wonder when you consider that God is the author!

So let's open our Bibles to read the greatest book ever written. We'll start in Genesis chapter 12.

## BRING IT UP

**(SCHOLAR)** How do you think God's covenant with Abraham fits into God's plan of salvation?

**(SCRIBE)** Why do you think God tells Abraham that he will be a "father of many nations"?

While you're turning there, remember that I asked if your favorite book had a central theme? In the Bible, the central theme is God's plan for salvation. While we read about what God wants us to do to be saved in the New Testament, the foundation of His plan is strongly rooted in the Old Testament, some 4,000 years before Jesus is born. We need to understand how the fascinating events and people of the Old Testament are directly related to the New Testament.

And so it starts in Genesis chapter 12, where God selects an upright, God-fearing man named Abram with whom He makes a covenant. A covenant is more than just a promise based on what you tell another person. Rather, a covenant is a promise of the highest standard based on how you live. As in the example of God and Abram, a covenant is usually two-sided, where both sides agree to do certain things that affect the other side.

### (READ GENESIS 12:1-3)

Here, God tells Abram to leave his homeland of Ur in Mesopotamia and head out to a land that He will give to him and later to his descendants. You may know that land is Canaan. God promises to make Abram a great nation and his name great, and that He will bless him and his descendants. That's what God promises Abram.

So, what does Abram promise God in return? God commands that Abram and his descendants be "blameless" (Deuteronomy 18:13). That's our Bible Word of the Day. To be blameless, however, does not mean that God commands perfection from Abram, but that he and his descendants should always strive toward the goal of holiness (Ephesians 1:4 commands Christians to be holy and blameless before Him in love). If they live like God wants them to, then Abram's family will be a blessing to "all the families of the earth" (Genesis 12:3).

God changes Abram's name to Abraham and tells him that he will be the "father of many nations" (Genesis 17:5-6).

### (READ GENESIS 17:7-8)

But, Abraham and his wife Sarah think they've hit a snag concerning God's promise: They have no children and they are old—really old. Sarah in particular is way past her childbearing years. How can Abraham have all these descendants when he doesn't even have a child with Sarah? The Bible says Abraham fell on his face and laughed and said in his heart, "Shall a child be born to a man who is one hundred years old? And shall Sarah, who is ninety years old, bear a child?" God assures Abraham that indeed Sarah will give birth to a son. Later, the Lord appears to Abraham again and reminds him that Sarah will have a son. Sarah, who's standing at the tent door behind her husband, overhears this

**WRITTEN FOR OUR LEARNING**

conversation. Her reaction?

## (READ GENESIS 18:12)

Then the Lord asks Abraham why Sarah laughed. God knows she laughed, but Sarah denies she laughed and tells God, "I did not laugh." God responds, "No, but you did laugh."

Because nothing is too hard for the Lord, He has the last laugh as Sarah gives birth to a son when Abraham is 100 years old.

## (READ GENESIS 21:6-7)

It's interesting to learn the meanings of many names in the Old Testament. The name *Isaac*, Abraham and Sarah's son in their old age, means "he laughs."

---

 **BIBLE BASICS:**

1. What does the word *Genesis* mean? **Beginnings**
2. Who does God select to be the "father of many nations?" **Abraham**
3. Who is Abraham's wife? **Sarah**
4. At different times, how do Abraham and Sarah react at the prospect of Sarah having a child in her old age? **They laugh.**
5. Where does Abraham leave to go where God says? **Ur in Mesopotamia**
6. Where does God tell Abraham to go? **Canaan**
7. What is the name of Abraham's and Sarah's son? **Isaac**
8. How old is Abraham when Isaac is born? **100 years old**
9. How old is Sarah when she gives birth to Isaac? **90 years old**
10. When God tells Abraham to go "to a land that I will show you," what country is it? **Canaan**
11. In addition to making Abraham a great nation, what else will God make great? **Abraham's name**
12. What does God command that Abraham and his descendants promise in return? **To be blameless and a blessing to others**

---

 **BESIDE THE POINT /**  **BRING IT HOME:**

(This lesson's activity combines both in-class participation and parental involvement at home.)

While genealogy is a popular hobby today, being able to trace one's lineage was serious business for the

Jews. The Jews knew their ancestors and were commonly identified according to their families.

**(SCHOLAR)** To help your students understand the concepts of generations, descendants, and ancestors, let them create their own family pedigrees. Blank, printable charts are available at no charge from several online sites and can be used for your students to fill in the names of their parents, grandparents, and great-grandparents. Get them started in class, listing their parents' names. Enlisting their parents' help, the students complete their trees as much as they can at home and bring them back to share their ancestral discoveries with their classmates. The birth and/or death dates on their own family trees gives them a visual understanding of generations and the passage of time, concepts that are somewhat abstract in their young minds.

As an alternative, because some children who are adopted or are foster children may not be able to complete the above assignment, you may prefer tracing the generations from Adam to Noah. It will be a neat way to show how many of the people in the beginning of the Old Testament would have been living at the same time.

**(SCRIBE)** The activity at this level is pared down so they can grasp all this. Explain to them what the word *ancestor* means: those who lived before a person—parent, grandparent, great-grandparent, etc. While you're at it, make sure they know a descendant is sort of the opposite: those who live after a person—child, grandchild, great-grandchild. Each person represents a generation. The best way to illustrate ancestors/descendants/generations is to draw it on the board for them to see. On one side, write Abraham and Sarah. Below their names, write Isaac as their son and below Isaac write Jacob and Esau and their grandsons. Above Abraham, write Terah as his father, and above Terah, Nahor as his grandfather (Genesis 11:24-27). On the other side of the board, write the same for you or someone they know that has children (to show at least one descendant level). Their **BRING IT HOME** assignment is to ask their parents for information for their own trees, such as grandparents' or great-grandparents' names. They can share what they learned during the next class.

---

  **BEYOND THE LESSON:**

**(SCHOLAR)** God makes another covenant with "a just man, perfect in his generations who walked with God" (Genesis 6:9). Who is this man and what is the covenant (Genesis 8:8-11)? What is the sign from God (Genesis 8:13-15)?

Answer: **Noah; that God will never destroy the earth by water again; rainbow.**

**(SCRIBE)** Luke 1:5-7 tells us of another couple, described as "righteous and blameless," who are old like Abraham and Sarah and are also told they will have a son. Who are they and what happens to the father when he does not believe the angel Gabriel's words (Luke 1:18-20)?

Answer: **Elizabeth and Zacharias, the parents of John the Baptist. Zacharias becomes mute until the child is born.**

# - LESSON 2 -
# ISAAC AND REBEKAH: A MARRIAGE MADE IN HEAVEN

Scripture Text: Genesis 24

 ## BEFORE THE EVENT:

Only 40 years pass between Isaac's birth and his marriage to Rebekah. But Genesis chapters 21 through 23 record a few events, including God's command to Abraham to sacrifice his young son Isaac as a burnt offering.

- Hagar's and Ishmael's Forced Departure (Genesis 21:8-21): Sarah tells Abraham to send away the woman she chose to bear a son for her husband well before Isaac was born. Hagar and the now teenage Ishmael leave but the Lord assures her that Ishmael, like Isaac, will become a great nation.
- Rebekah's Family (Genesis 22:20-23): The genealogy of Rebekah, Isaac's wife, is recorded here.
- Sarah's Death and Burial (Genesis 23): Sarah dies at 127 and is buried in the same cave in which Abraham will later be buried.

 ## LESSON:

Although she is old enough to be his great-grandmother, Sarah gives birth to Isaac, just as God promises. A birth of a baby is always a joyous occasion, but Isaac's birth is extra special because of God's covenant with Abraham that through him all nations will be blessed. Not only will Abraham be blessed with many descendants, but, more importantly, one of those descendants will be the Messiah, Jesus, who is born about 1,900 years after Isaac is born.

So imagine how Abraham feels when one day God tells him to kill Isaac and sacrifice him as a burnt offering. Abraham knows about burnt offerings because worship to God often involves killing an animal, such as a lamb, and using fire on an altar to burn it. Even though God tells him to kill his precious child, Abraham doesn't argue with God, and he doesn't even question God. Rather, because of his faith in God, Abraham sets out to do exactly what God has commanded him. He binds his son and places him upon an altar. As Abraham stretches out his hand to slay the boy with a knife, an Angel of the Lord stops him. Then, Abraham sees a ram caught in a thicket by its horns, which replaces his son as the burnt offering. The Bible says this was God's test of Abraham's faith

 ## BIBLE WORD OF THE DAY:

SEED

Definition: A person's children, descendants, offspring (Genesis 21:12).

"*He shall see His **seed**, He shall prolong His days, and the pleasure of the Lord shall prosper in His hand*" (Isaiah 53:10).

## BIBLE VERSES

Genesis 24:12-14
Genesis 24:17-19
Genesis 24:58

 ## BIG IDEA

**(SCHOLAR)** Let God through His Word guide you when you select a husband or wife.

**(SCRIBE)** Like Rebekah, we need to obey God now, not later.

(Genesis 22:1).

Isaac grows up and marries a beautiful woman named Rebekah (Genesis 24:15). She's not just any woman. Rebekah is specifically chosen for Isaac as part of God's divine plan to fulfill His covenant with Abraham. Isaac and Rebekah's marriage is an arranged marriage, which means the parents select their children's husbands and wives. Except in this case, God does the selecting.

It begins when an aging Abraham sends his oldest servant who rules over his house to find a wife for Isaac, and not just any wife, either. Abraham carefully instructs the servant not to take a woman from Canaan, who worships false gods. But instead he tells the servant to return to his country and bring back a wife from his family. The servant knows this is a lot of responsibility, but Abraham reassures him that God will guide him on his journey to select a wife for Isaac. So with ten of his master's camels in tow, the servant heads out to the land of Mesopotamia where Abraham lived before God told him to go Canaan. Outside the city of Nahor, the servant and the camels stop beside a well of water. It's evening, the time when the women of the city usually go to the well to draw water. And it's a good time for Abraham's servant to seek God's direction.

## BRING IT UP

**(SCHOLAR)** In what ways is the servant a good example for us to follow today?

**(SCRIBE)** Why do you think the servant is so eager and excited to tell others about his story to find a wife for Isaac?

## (READ GENESIS 24:12-14)

Pretty simple. The servant will just need to recognize the sign. That is, the woman who offers a drink of water to both him and the camels is the one God wants as a wife for Isaac. Before the servant can even finish speaking, Rebekah appears with her water pitcher in hand.

## (READ GENESIS 24:17-19)

The servant immediately knows that Rebekah is the one and gives her a golden nose ring and two bracelets as he asks her about her family and about a place to spend the night. Rebekah says her father is Bethuel and that they have a place for them to stay. The servant bows and worships the Lord, saying that He led him to his master Abraham's family.

Rebekah runs and tells her family, including her brother Laban. After welcoming the servant to their home, Laban takes care of the camels and offers a meal to the servant. But the servant is so excited about how the Lord has taken care of him and his master Abraham that he can't eat until he tells his story, which he does with enthusiasm (Genesis 24: 34-49). When the servant finishes his story, Laban realizes this is from God and allows his sister to go back with Abraham's servant. However, Laban wants Rebekah stay with her family for a few more days before going to Canaan to be Isaac's wife. It's an understandable request since all of this is sudden and the family wants a chance to spend some time with her before she departs to another country. But Abraham's servant insists that they leave now. So they ask Rebekah herself.

## (READ GENESIS 24:58)

There's no time like the present, and Rebekah clearly wants to obey God. So the servant and Rebekah leave immediately. When they arrive at Isaac's home in Canaan, Rebekah gets the first glimpse of her future husband in the field. The servant tells Isaac "all the things that he had done" in order to bring Rebekah home to him. You can imagine the servant's excitement when he tells his story again!

## BIBLE BASICS:

1. Who is 127 years old when she dies? **Sarah**
2. Who does Abraham send to get a wife for Isaac? **His oldest servant**
3. Where may the servant not go to choose a wife? **Canaan**
4. Where is the servant to go to choose a wife? **Abraham's home, Mesopotamia**
5. To what kind of animal does Rebekah offer a drink of water? **Camel**
6. Who is Rebekah's brother? **Laban**
7. What does the servant do when Laban agrees to allow his sister to go with him? **Worships the Lord**
8. Where does Abraham live at this time? **Canaan**
9. Who did Abraham say will guide his servant to choose a wife for Isaac? **God who will send an angel**
10. What was Rebekah doing when the servant saw her? **Drawing water**
11. What does the servant give Rebekah after the camels finished drinking? **A golden nose ring and two bracelets**
12. To whom does the servant retell his story of how he chose a wife for Isaac? **Laban and Isaac**

## BESIDE THE POINT:

**(SCRIBE & SCHOLAR)** Even though Isaac did not personally select Rebekah as his wife, the two enjoyed a long, successful marriage. Such arranged marriages are not common in this country, where men and women date (or in the olden days, court) each other for a period of time before marrying. During this time, the couple finds out as much as they can about each other—their beliefs, their viewpoints, their personalities, their education, their likes and dislikes, etc.—before making a decision regarding a lifelong commitment with each other. Determining who you will marry is one of the most important choices you will make in life, and God expects you to take it seriously.

Invite a respected, older couple from your congregation who would be willing to impart their wisdom to your students on the subject of a lasting, God-centered marriage. Inform the couple that their guest appearance in your class is related to the story of Isaac and Rebekah so they can prepare their discussion. Also, prepare your students for their arrival to your class, helping them write a few questions for the couple. Afterwards, the class should write a thank you note to the couple, expressing appreciation for their visit and their time.

 **BRING IT HOME:**

**(SCHOLAR)** The students ask their parents, "What three qualities do you want my future husband or wife to have?" By this the students know that, although their parents probably won't go out and pick their future spouses, their parents, like Abraham, deeply care about the kind of person they will marry.

**(SCRIBE)** The students ask their parents, "What kind of person does God want us to marry?" By this the students know they can always go to the Bible to find out His will for them.

---

 **BEYOND THE LESSON:**

**(SCHOLAR)** The Bible does not often comment on a person's outer beauty, such as Sarah (Genesis 12:11) and Rebekah (Genesis 24:16). Name the three people whose outward appearance is recorded in Genesis 29:17, Genesis 39:6, and 1 Samuel 16:12.

Answer: **Rachel, Joseph, and David.**

**(SCRIBE)** After Abraham dies, Old Testament prophets repeatedly remind his descendants about God's covenant to them and about the coming Messiah through his seed. Read Micah 5:2. More than 700 years before Christ is born, the prophet reveals the city Christ will be born in. What is it?

Answer: **Bethlehem**

## - LESSON 3 -
# JACOB AND ESAU: FIGHTING AND FORGIVING BROTHERS

Scripture Text: Genesis 25:19-34, 27; 33:1-17

 ## BEFORE THE EVENT:

Only 20 years or so pass between the marriage of Isaac and Rebekah and the birth of their twins, Jacob and Esau.

- **Abraham's New Wife (Genesis 25:1-6):** After Sarah's death a few years earlier, Abraham takes another wife named Keturah and he has more sons by her.
- **Abraham's Death (Genesis 25:7-11):** The father of all nations dies at age 175, and his sons, Isaac and Ishmael, bury him in the cave of Machpelah where Sarah is buried.

 ## LESSON:

When Isaac is 60 years old, Rebekah becomes pregnant with twins. Something doesn't feel right with the pregnancy, so she prays to God.

### (READ GENESIS 25:22-23)

Rebekah is an example of how we should take our problems to God in prayer. Anyway, these baby boys who are battling inside Rebekah's womb make their entry into the world in an interesting fashion. The first, named Esau, comes out red and looks like a hairy piece of cloth. His not-so-hairy twin brother Jacob comes out grabbing Esau's heel, as if they were continuing their wrestling match while traveling down the birth canal.

You probably know some twins who have personalities as different as night and day. This is true of Jacob and Esau. Esau likes being outside where he spends most of his time hunting wild animals while the mild-mannered Jacob prefers being inside the tents tending to chores closer to home. As a result, Jacob becomes Rebekah's favorite son while Isaac and Esau are close because of their bond of hunting. Not surprisingly, this sets the stage for some classic sibling rivalry. And this struggle between the brothers has a direct impact on the course of God's covenant with the boys' grandfather Abraham.

 ## BIBLE WORD OF THE DAY:

DECEIT

Definition: Act that conceals, covers up, or misrepresents the truth (Genesis 27:35).

*"Deceit is in the heart of those who devise evil, but counselors of peace have joy"* (Proverbs 12:20).

## BIBLE VERSES

Genesis 25:22-23
Genesis 27:11-12
Genesis 33:4

 ## BIG IDEA

**(SCHOLAR)** God commands us to forgive others, which is much better than holding on to a grudge.

**(SCRIBE)** Forgive others because God forgives you.

### JACOB AND ESAU: FIGHTING AND FORGIVING BROTHERS

One day, Jacob cooks a stew, and Esau, after a long day of hunting in the field, comes inside tired and hungry. Very hungry. So he asks his brother for some of that stew because he's so weary. Jacob takes advantage of his brother's weak condition and tells him he will be glad to give him stew… on the condition he sell his birthright to him. Esau tells his younger brother that his birthright is worthless to him if he dies from starvation. So he gives Jacob his birthright for a bowl of stew.

In other words, God's covenant to Abraham means nothing to Esau who would rather eat a bowl of stew than be a part of that promise which is his birthright as the older son. His birthright is not the only thing Esau loses to Jacob, who tricks their father Isaac into giving him the blessing meant for Esau. Jacob has help in tricking Isaac—his mother Rebekah.

Rebekah overhears old, blind Isaac telling Esau to hunt an animal from which to make some savory food for him to eat and then bless him before he dies. So while Esau is out of the house doing what his father asks, Rebekah takes advantage this time and concocts a plan to deceive Isaac into thinking he's blessing Esau, the older son, when he is really blessing Jacob, the younger. Rebekah gives Jacob the backstory and then instructs her favorite son to kill two young goats so she can prepare some delicious food for Isaac. The plan is for Jacob to pretend to be Esau and serve the food to Isaac. Remember that Isaac is old and can barely see so maybe Jacob could get away with it. Unless he gets too close.

## BRING IT UP

**(SCHOLAR)** Why do you think God allowed all the lies and deceptions that resulted in Esau's loss of his birthright and blessing?

**(SCRIBE)** What do you think about Rebekah's role in deceiving Esau?

## (READ GENESIS 27:11-12)

Good point. So Rebekah takes clothes worn by Esau that have a rustic, outdoorsy smell and puts them on Jacob. Further, she takes the skins of those two young goats and puts them on Jacob's hands and the smooth part of his neck for added deception. With the savory food in hand, Jacob puts into action the plan to steal Esau's blessing.

Looking and smelling like Esau, Jacob brings Isaac the savory food and tricks Isaac into believing he's Esau. So thinking he is blessing Esau, Isaac actually blesses Jacob, inadvertently making the younger son the heir of God's promise to Abraham a couple of hundred years earlier. Isaac is barely finished blessing Jacob when Esau walks in with his own savory food to serve his father and receive his blessing. How do you think Esau reacts when Isaac tells him what happened?

Isaac cannot take back the blessing he gave to Jacob, but he does give Esau a smaller blessing. Remember God tells Rebekah when she's still pregnant with the twins that the older will serve the younger? This prophecy now comes to pass when Isaac blesses them. Esau hates Jacob so much he wants to kill him and intends to do so after Isaac dies. Rebekah gets wind of this and makes arrangements for her favorite son to flee to her brother Laban's house until Esau calms down. Before he leaves, Isaac tells Jacob to not take a wife from Canaan and instead take one from the daughters of Laban.

Many years pass and a lot has happened in Jacob's life, including his marriage to two of Laban's daughters, Leah and Rachel, and the births of 11 sons. (The twelfth son, Benjamin, is born a short time later, and Rachel dies in childbirth.) Jacob's name is also changed to Israel (Genesis 32:28). Then the estranged brothers finally come face to face. Naturally, Jacob is scared and prepares for the worst because the last he heard, his brother wanted to kill him for stealing the family inheritance. Jacob expects Esau to want revenge and prays to God for protection. After bowing to the ground seven times as he greets Esau, Jacob does not expect what happens next.

### (READ GENESIS 33:4)

Jacob is sorry for cheating and mistreating his brother, and Esau responds with grace and mercy. He forgives Jacob when he least expects or deserves it. This is what God does for us when we are sorry. Jacob tries to make it up to Esau by offering him gifts, which Esau initially refuses but later accepts. The two then have a happy family reunion!

---

## BIBLE BASICS:

1. When does the fighting between Jacob and Esau start? **In their mother's womb**
2. Who is older, Jacob or Esau? **Esau**
3. What two things does Jacob take from Esau? **His birthright and blessing**
4. How does Esau react when he discovers Jacob's "trick"? **He cried bitterly and exceedingly at first; he then hated Jacob so much he intended to kill him**
5. Where does Jacob go to escape Esau's wrath? **Laban's house**
6. Who are the two daughters of Laban that Jacob marries? **Leah and Rachel**
7. How many times does Jacob bow to Esau? **Seven**
8. When the twins struggle within her, what does Rebekah do? **Pray**
9. When God tells Rebekah that two nations are in her womb, what will the older do to the younger? **Serve him**
10. Who is Jacob's and Esau's grandfather? **Abraham**
11. Why can't Isaac tell which twin is which unless he touches their skin? **He's old and cannot see**
12. What does Jacob wear to make his father think he's Esau? **Esau's clothes and goat skins on his hands and his neck**

---

## BESIDE THE POINT:

**(SCHOLAR)** Read Jesus' parable of The Unmerciful Servant in Matthew 18:21-35 with the class. Jesus tells this parable in response to Peter's question about how often someone is required to forgive a brother. Peter guesses that it might be up to seven times, but Jesus says to forgive up to seventy times seven. Ask the class what Jesus means by "up to seventy times seven." Then, discuss the parable, mainly the servant and his role as the forgiven at the beginning. Why do you think the servant refuses to forgive a fellow servant later on? Suggest that the servant does not appreciate the forgiveness he received from his master because if he did, then he would have passed on that spirit of forgiveness to the other servant. Through God's plan of salvation God forgives our sins, and if we do not forgive those who sin against us, then we fail to appreciate the full value of Jesus' sacrifice on the cross.

### JACOB AND ESAU: FIGHTING AND FORGIVING BROTHERS

(**SCRIBE**) Anyone with a brother or sister can certainly relate on some level to the sibling squabbles of Jacob and Esau. Because this lesson focuses on forgiveness, it's a good time to allow your students to talk about a specific conflict with their brother or sister (or friend if the student doesn't have either) in which the student forgave the sibling. Ask the student whether he/she felt better after he/she forgave the sibling. Allow time for other students to do the same, and come to a class conclusion that it's always better to forgive your brother.

##  BRING IT HOME:

(**SCHOLAR & SCRIBE**) Ask your students to make a concentrated effort this week to forgive any family member who does something against them. If that family member doesn't know they've hurt them, encourage your students to go and talk with the person, always being ready to forgive. Explain to your students that forgiveness means they no longer hold the wrong doing to the account of the family member. It will be tough to forget; however, they must not allow the offense to prevent them from extending forgiveness like God does for us upon repentance and seeking forgiveness. Remind them how forgiving others is not only a command from God but it also makes them feel better..

##  BEYOND THE LESSON:

(**SCHOLAR**) We just studied about Jacob's repentance and Esau's forgiveness. However, Esau's descendants, called Edomites, apparently prefer to keep the family feud going hundreds of years later. When Jacob's descendants fall on hard times such as being attacked by foreign armies, Esau's descendants seem flat-out happy about their cousins' misfortunes and difficulties. They enjoy kicking their cousins when they're down. This goes on for many years, and in Obadiah, the shortest book in the Old Testament, we read what God plans to do about it. In the book of Obadiah, God says He will destroy the house of Esau. In verse 18, what specifically will Esau's house become?

Answer: **Stubble**

(**SCRIBE**) The Bible records only three cases of twins. Besides Jacob and Esau, there is Jacob's grandsons, Perez and Zerah, whose unusual births are recorded in Genesis 38:27-30. According to Ruth 4:18, which twin is an ancestor of David? Also, in John 20:24, which of Jesus' disciples is known as "The Twin"?

Answer: **Perez; Thomas**

# - LESSON 4 -
# JOSEPH: SERVING GOD IN AFFLICTION

Scripture Text: Genesis 37, 39, 40, 41, 42:1-52

##  BEFORE THE EVENT:

A few of the major events in Jacob's life that precede the lesson include his marriages and the births of his 12 sons.

- Jacob and Laban (Genesis 29): Jacob makes a deal with Laban to work seven years to marry his daughter Rachel. He gets big sister Leah instead and ends up working another seven years for the love of his life.
- First of Twelve Sons of Israel Born (Genesis 29:31-35): The unloved Leah gives birth to firstborn son Reuben. Next come Simeon, Levi, and Judah, all with Leah.
- The Rest of the Sons of Israel Born (Genesis 30:1-24; 35:16-20): Dan and Naphtali (with Rachel's maid Bilhah), Gad and Asher (with Leah's maid Zilpah), Issachar and Zebulun (with Leah) and Joseph and Benjamin (with Rachel). Rachel dies while giving birth to the youngest son Benjamin.
- Jacob Settles in Canaan (Genesis 33:18-20): After his meeting with Esau, Jacob arrives safely at Shechem in the land of Canaan.
- Death of Isaac (Genesis 35:27-29): Isaac dies at age 180 and his sons Jacob and Esau bury him.

##  LESSON:

No family is perfect. And the family God promised Abraham would become great is not perfect—far from it. Less than 200 years after God's covenant with Abraham, issues from jealousy to division are tearing the family apart. Among them: two of Jacob's (now called Israel) sons, Judah and Simeon, leave the family, taking pagan wives from Canaan, which are forbidden because they worship false gods. Israel's wives Leah and Rachel are constantly at odds because of their jealousy toward each other.

And most notably, Israel's 11th son Joseph is the target of intense scorn and hatred from his older brothers because of jealousy. The brothers want to kill Joseph but settle for pawning him off as a slave to the Midianites for 20 shekels of silver (Genesis 37:28). Showing him Joseph's torn, blood-dipped tunic, the brothers convince an aging Israel that Joseph was

---

## BIBLE WORD OF THE DAY:

AFFLICTION

Definition: A cause of pain or suffering (Genesis 41:52).

*"For the Lord saw that the **affliction** of Israel was very bitter..."* (2 Kings 14:26).

## BIBLE VERSES

Genesis 39:3-5
Genesis 39:21
Genesis 41:32
Genesis 41:37-38

## BIG IDEA

**(SCHOLAR & SCRIBE)** In good times and bad, our behavior should always glorify God.

**(SCHOLAR & SCRIBE)** As long as we are faithful to Him, God will use our lives for good.

mauled to death by a wild beast. Israel is in such anguish that no one is able to comfort him as he mourns the loss of his favorite son.

Who will restore this family that is falling apart and shape it into a great nation? God. And He will do it through Joseph. And it will take about 20 years. At this point, Joseph is an 18-year-old Egyptian slave. Because God is with Joseph, he is not a common slave, laboring in the field or in construction. He is sold to a rich Egyptian official Potiphar.

### BRING IT UP

**(SCHOLAR & SCRIBE)** Why is Joseph's life so important, and what is his impact on God's covenant with Abraham?

### (READ GENESIS 39:3-5)

After his promotion as overseer of his house, Potiphar's wife repeatedly attempts to cause Joseph to sin against God. When Joseph refuses to give in to her demands, she becomes angry. To get back at Joseph, she falsely accuses Joseph of betraying Potiphar. In the end, Potiphar believes his lying wife and sends Joseph to prison.

### (READ GENESIS 39:21)

God never leaves Joseph who remains faithful to God in spite of his circumstances, first as a slave and now a prisoner. While in prison, he glorifies God who gives him the ability to interpret the dreams of the chief baker and the chief butler, two fellow prisoners. Both of these interpretations come to pass, resulting in the death of the baker and the release of the butler. Two years later, Pharaoh has a disturbing dream. Twice. None of Pharaoh's advisors or wise men can figure out what the dream means. It just so happens that Joseph's old prison pal the butler learns about Pharaoh's problem and tells Pharaoh about Joseph and his dream interpretation skills. Pharoah sends for Joseph in prison, and up front Joseph tells Pharaoh that the interpretation is from God not him.

After hearing the details of the dream involving seven fat cows and seven ugly gaunt cows, Joseph says, "God has shown Pharaoh what He is about to do." In other words, God has enabled Joseph to reveal the meaning of dreams, but that same God controls all things. In this case, God controls the next seven years when there will be plenty of crops and the seven years after that when a severe famine will arise in Egypt. Joseph explains why Pharaoh's dream occurred two times.

### (READ GENESIS 41:32)

Joseph advises Pharaoh to prepare for the upcoming famine, to store away grain during the plentiful years so that there will be enough food during the famine. He suggests appointing an exceedingly wise man to be in charge, making sure that they collect one-fifth of the grain produced to cover the famine years.

### (READ GENESIS 41:37-38)

Pharaoh then appoints an exceedingly wise man, Joseph, as governor over all the land of Egypt, second only to the Pharaoh himself. Joseph is 30 at the beginning of the seven years of plenty when he "gathered very much grain, as the sand of the sea, until he stopped counting, for it was immeasurable." Also, during this time he marries Asenath, with whom he has two sons: Manasseh, "For God has made me forget all my toil and all my father's house;" and Ephraim, "For God has caused me to be fruitful in the land of my affliction."

 **BIBLE BASICS:**

1. How many sons does Jacob (Israel) have? **12**
2. Who is Israel's favorite son? **Joseph**
3. For how much do the brothers receive for selling Joseph to slave traders? **20 shekels of silver**
4. Why does Israel think Joseph is dead? **Because his sons showed him Joseph's torn coat covered with blood**
5. How old is Joseph when he is sold to the Midianites? **18**
6. In whose house does Joseph work as an overseer? **Potiphar**
7. For what two people does Joseph interpret their dreams in prison? **Chief baker and chief butler**
8. How many years after the chief butler is released from prison does Pharaoh have the dream of fat, skinny, and ugly cows? **Two**
9. Who tells Pharaoh about Joseph's ability to interpret dreams? **Chief butler**
10. What does Pharaoh's dream mean? **That there will be seven years of plentiful harvest followed by seven years of severe famine**
11. How old is Joseph when Pharaoh appoints him as second-in-command in Egypt? **30**
12. When his son Ephraim is born, Joseph says that he has been what in the land of his affliction? **Fruitful**

 **BESIDE THE POINT:**

**(SCHOLAR)** Jacob has 12 sons whose descendants become known as the Israelites, God's chosen people. In this lesson, they are responsible for selling their brother Joseph into slavery, propelling a series of events that will impact their entire family and the future of God's covenant with their ancestor Abraham. Say which son each of the following statements describe:

1. The oldest son and the one who convinces his brothers not to kill Joseph and put him in a pit instead (Genesis 37:22). **Reuben**
2. The second- and third-oldest sons and the ones who destroy Shechem for the sake of their sister Dinah (Genesis 34:25-26). **Levi and Simeon**
3. The son who is an ancestor of Moses (Exodus 6:16-20). **Levi**
4. The fourth son and the one who has the idea to sell Joseph to the Midianite slave traders rather than let him die in the pit (Genesis 37:27). **Judah**
5. Two sons whose families are the brave soldiers in the Song of Deborah during the battle against Sisera (Judges 5:18). **Zebulun and Naphtali**
6. The youngest son born to Rachel who died giving birth to him (Genesis 35:16-19). **Benjamin**

**JOSEPH: SERVING GOD IN AFFLICTION**

**(SCRIBE)** Test the students' knowledge of Joseph by having them answer the following bold italicized words:

Joseph is the 11th son of Jacob, and his mother is _Rachel_. Rachel later has Jacob's 12th son, whose name is _Benjamin_. Jacob, called Israel, loves Joseph more than all his children because he is the son of his old _age_. Israel shows his love for his favorite son by giving him a _coat of many colors_. Joseph also has _dreams_, which depict him reigning over his brothers. In one dream, the _sun_, the _moon_, and the 11 _stars_ bow down to him. This makes his brothers angry and jealous. The brothers first decide to _kill_ Joseph but after _Reuben_ intercedes, they decide to cast Joseph into a _pit_. Then _Judah_ has the idea to sell Joseph to Midianite slave traders. The brothers let their father think _Joseph_ is dead, however, by showing Israel Joseph's coat that they dipped in goat's _blood_.

As a slave, Joseph is taken down to _Egypt_. He works for _Potiphar_, an officer of Pharaoh. Joseph is described as _handsome_ in appearance. Potiphar's wife becomes interested in Joseph but Joseph refuses to sin against _God_. Potiphar's wife is not happy and decides to get Joseph in trouble with Potiphar. As a result, Joseph is thrown in _prison_.

As a prisoner, Joseph is given responsibility of authority over the other _prisoners_. One prisoner, the chief _baker_ has a dream about a vine with three branches, and another prisoner, the chief _butler_, has a dream about three white baskets on his head. Joseph, who says interpretations are from _God_, tells them the meanings of their dreams. In the end, the butler is _released_ from prison and returned to his position, and the baker is _hanged_ on a tree. Pharaoh later has a dream, and the _butler_ remembers Joseph in prison and tells Pharoah that Joseph can interpret it. Explaining that _God_ will give Pharaoh an answer of peace, Joseph tells him what his dream of _seven_ fat cows and _seven_ ugly, skinny cows means. The seven fat cows represent _seven_ years of plenty, and the seven thin and ugly cows represent seven years of _famine_. Joseph then tells Pharaoh to prepare for the _famine_ during the seven years of plenty by appointing a wise man to oversee officers in order to collect one-fifth of the grain and store it for use during the _plentiful years_. Pharaoh selects _Joseph_ for that job, promoting him as second in all of Egypt next to Pharaoh.

# BRING IT HOME:

**(SCHOLAR & SCRIBE)** To get a hint of what happens next, ask your parent to read with you the portion of Stephen's sermon about Joseph, including what happens when the famine arrives and so do Joseph's long-lost brothers (Acts 7:9-16).

# BEYOND THE LESSON:

**(SCHOLAR & SCRIBE)** Read Matthew 1:1-3. Which of Jacob's sons is listed as a direct ancestor of Jesus?

Answer: **Judah**

**(SCHOLAR & SCRIBE)** Read Genesis 12:10. Shortly after receiving God's covenant, Abraham (then still called

**WRITTEN FOR OUR LEARNING**

Abram) arrives in Canaan. But he then goes to Egypt. Why?

Answer: **Because there was a severe famine in the land**

**WRITTEN FOR OUR LEARNING**

# - LESSON 5 -
# JOSEPH: BLESSINGS THROUGH GOD'S PROVIDENCE

Scripture Text: Genesis 42–47

## BEFORE THE EVENT:

Joseph is one of the most well-known personalities in the Bible, spanning 12 of the last 13 chapters in the book of Genesis. In 110 years, Joseph leads a fascinating life chock full of adventures, each illustrating a remarkable example of his unwavering faith in God. This lesson continues where Lesson 4 ends: Pharaoh appoints Joseph as second in charge over the land of Egypt in preparation of the famine due to occur in seven years. Lesson 5 begins with the reappearance of his brothers who come to Egypt to buy grain because of the famine. As a review, here's a brief look at the events leading to this point in time.

- Joseph Dreams of Greatness (Genesis 37:1-10): Joseph at 17 has dreams indicating that one day his brothers, as well as his parents, will bow down to him.
- Joseph's Brothers Sell the "Dreamer" (Genesis 37:12-36): The brothers' jealousy of their little brother get the best of them and end up selling him into slavery instead of killing him. However, Jacob believes he's dead.
- Joseph Becomes a Slave in Potiphar's House (Genesis 39): After refusing to sin against God with Potiphar's wife, Joseph finds himself in prison.
- Joseph Interprets the Baker's and Butler's Dreams (Genesis 40): Pharaoh's servants have dreams, and Joseph tells them their meanings.
- Joseph Interprets Pharaoh's Dreams (Genesis 41:1-52): Pharaoh dreams the same dream twice about the upcoming famine, which Joseph interprets, provides advice and becomes second-in-command in Egypt.
- The Famine Begins (Genesis 41:53-57): The famine is severe across the land, and people from all countries come to Joseph in Egypt to buy grain.

## LESSON:

When we left Joseph last week, he was the ruler of Egypt, second-in-command only to Pharaoh himself, and was making

## BIBLE WORD OF THE DAY:

FAMINE

Definition: Extreme shortage of food (Genesis 42:5).

"…I will increase the *famine* upon you and cut off your supply of bread" (Ezekiel 5:16).

## BIBLE VERSES

Genesis 42:6-8
Genesis 42:20-21
Genesis 42:36
Genesis 45:7-8

## BIG IDEA

**(SCHOLAR & SCRIBE)** God took care of Abraham's descendants in the Old Testament, and He takes care of Christians today.

**(SCHOLAR)** Through Joseph, God reunited His people and reaffirmed the continuance of

*(continued on next page…)*

preparations for the famine. The famine is severe, affecting "all the face of the earth," and folks from all countries come to Joseph in Egypt to buy grain (Genesis 41:56-57). Ten of those folks include Joseph's brothers, who travel about 200 miles from Canaan to Egypt to buy grain from Joseph, except they don't know he's Joseph.

## (READ GENESIS 42:6-8)

Remember, Joseph is around 37 years old now. He was 18 when his brothers last saw him being carried away to a foreign country by slave traders. So, naturally, his appearance has changed a lot. And because he's been living in Egypt a long time, he now looks and sounds like an Egyptian. Besides, for all they know, Joseph is dead. So Joseph is the last person they'd expect to see selling grain as the top ruler in Egypt. But when Joseph sees and recognizes his brothers who just bowed down to him, he immediately remembers his dreams that predicted he would someday rule over his brothers. His long-ago dreams are now reality, made to happen through the providence of God. Providence is simply God's protective care of His people. Time and time again, no matter where Joseph finds himself, he never doubts God and remains faithful to him. So, God provides for him and guides his rise to power in a foreign country. Because of the famine, Joseph's position as Egypt's governor allows him to save his family both physically from starvation and spiritually by bringing them together again. God is always in control, and all things work together for good to those who love God (Romans 8:28).

His covenant with Abraham.

**(SCRIBE)** Our love for God allows us to forgive others.

## BRING IT UP

**(SCHOLAR)** How do the events of Joseph's life reflect Romans 8:28?

**(SCRIBE)** What are some things Joseph does throughout his life that

Anyway, back to Joseph and his brothers. Instead of immediately revealing himself to his brothers who had treated him so harshly, separated him from his beloved family and at one point considered killing him, Joseph is rough on them. He tests them to see if they've changed for the better. So he accuses them of being spies and sees how they react. He knows they're not spies, but this way he finds out information about their family. By "tricking" them, Joseph learns whether he can trust his brothers now before he reveals himself to them. And it will take a little time because then Joseph demands to see Benjamin, the brother who did not make the trip to Egypt with them. To ensure they do so, Joseph ties up Simeon, the second-oldest brother, and holds him as a prisoner until they return to Egypt with his brother Benjamin.

## (READ GENESIS 42:20-21)

In essence, the brothers believe this is their punishment for the way they treated Joseph. Reuben, the oldest of the 12, reminds them how he told them not to kill Joseph. Joseph, of course, understands every word they're saying about what they think happened to him and turns away and weeps because he's so touched.

So they leave Egypt having gotten themselves in a big mess. First, they believe this harsh Egyptian ruler will kill them if they do not return with Benjamin, and second, they know their father will be very upset when they tell him that a foreign ruler demands to see Benjamin. The reason Benjamin is not with them on this trip is because Jacob feared for this son's safety. To make matters worse, when they arrive in Canaan, they discover their grain money in each of their sacks, causing them to be even more afraid. Is the governor of Egypt going to think they stole the money? No, because it is the governor of Egypt who put it there to begin with. But of course, they don't know that yet.

As expected, Jacob is overwhelmed with grief over the events in Egypt.

## (READ GENESIS 42:36)

Judah also steps up and tells Jacob that he will personally protect their youngest brother. Jacob realizes he must allow Benjamin to return with them to Egypt and instructs his sons to not only restore the money meant to pay for the grain the first trip but also to double the amount. Joseph greets them upon their return with Benjamin in tow and asks whether their father is alive and well. Once again, his brothers bow down to Joseph. He then sees Benjamin for the first time in 20 years, evoking such heartfelt emotions for his beloved brother that he dashes out of the room to weep alone. Later, they have a meal together and Joseph ensures Benjamin receives five times the amount of food as everyone else. Soon, they are on the road back to Canaan when Joseph's servants track them down, accuse them of being evil, and check out the brothers' sacks. Inside Benjamin's sack is Joseph's silver cup. Did Benjamin steal it? No, Joseph purposely put it there to bring them back to Egypt so he could "deal with" the one who "stole" it. The brothers are overwhelmed with grief wondering what's going to happen to Benjamin. Desperate to save Benjamin's life, Judah begs Joseph to not hurt Benjamin for their father's sake and then offers to take Benjamin's place by becoming Joseph's slave. Judah's willingness to sacrifice himself to save his brother proves his brothers' remorse to Joseph and how their hearts are turned back to God. He finally reveals himself to his brothers, and, when they are convinced, Joseph explains the events in his life that led up to this moment.

## (READ GENESIS 45:7-8)

Not surprisingly, when the brothers return to Jacob with the happy news that Joseph is alive, he is stunned and "his heart stood still" because he doesn't believe them. After they revived him, he becomes convinced. Then God tells Jacob it's okay for him to go to Egypt and that he'll see Joseph before he dies. Sixty-six members of Jacob's family, including his daughters-in-law and grandchildren, travel to Egypt to meet Joseph. Add Jacob, Joseph, and Joseph's two sons Ephraim and Manasseh, and the total is 70. Pharaoh sees to it that Joseph's family settles in Goshen, the best of the land in Egypt.

---

 **BIBLE BASICS:**

1. Why do Joseph's brothers go to Egypt? **To buy grain because of the famine**
2. Which brother does not go to Egypt the first time to buy grain? **Benjamin**
3. About how old is Benjamin when Joseph is sold into slavery? **10**
4. In Genesis 42:14, what does Joseph accuse his brothers of being? **Spies**
5. Whom does Joseph want to see and asks his brothers to bring to him? **Benjamin**
6. What will not happen to the brothers if they bring their youngest brother to Joseph? **They will not die**
7. Which brother is held as Joseph's prisoner until they return with Benjamin? **Simeon**
8. When the brothers notice that some money is in one of the sacks, how do they react? **They are afraid**

## JOSEPH: BLESSINGS THROUGH GOD'S PROVIDENCE

9. Which brother assures Jacob that he will allow his own two sons to be killed if he doesn't bring Benjamin back safely? **Reuben**

10. At the meal, how much more is Benjamin's serving compared to that of his brothers? **Five times**

11. What is put in Benjamin's sack before they depart for Canaan? **Joseph's silver cup**

12. Where does Joseph's family settle? **Goshen**

---

## BESIDE THE POINT:

**(SCHOLAR)** Many verses in this lesson reveal that Joseph is a man who weeps or cries in touching situations, such as when he first sees his brothers (Genesis 42:24) and when he first sees Benjamin (Genesis 43:30). The Bible contains many events of other tender-hearted men who weep for a variety of reasons. Look up the Scriptures below and identify the weeping man (or men) and the reason or the circumstance behind the emotion:

+ 1 Samuel 20:41—**David and Jonathan, loyal friends who remain such in spite of difficult circumstances**

+ 2 Kings 8:11—**Elisha, the prophet who is upset over the suffering that Hazael, king of Syria, will bring upon Israel**

+ 2 Kings 20:3—**Hezekiah, Judah's king who prays and weeps after learning about his illness**

+ Nehemiah 1:4—**Nehemiah, the civil governor of Jerusalem during the Babylonian Exile who mourns many days about Jerusalem's lack of a wall to protect it**

+ Job 30:25—**Job, God's suffering servant of God who says he has wept for others and wonders why God doesn't sympathize for him**

**(SCRIBE)** Put these highlights in Joseph's life in chronological order:

_____Reuben persuades his brothers not to kill Joseph. (**3**)
_____Joseph works as an overseer in Potiphar's house. (**5**)
_____Judah promises Israel that he will keep Benjamin safe upon returning to Egypt. (**11**)
_____Severe famine affects all of the lands. (**8**)
_____Simeon stays behind with Joseph until his brothers return with Benjamin. (**10**)
_____Rachel gives birth to Joseph. (**1**)
_____God tells Israel that it's okay to go to Egypt. (**15**)
_____Joseph's silver cup is discovered in Benjamin's sack. (**13**)
_____Joseph has a dream in which the sun, the moon, and the 11 stars bow down to him. (**2**)
_____Israel thinks his favorite son is dead when he sees Joseph's blood-soaked tunic. (**4**)
_____Joseph invites his brothers to eat with him and gives Benjamin five times the portion of food. (**12**)
_____Joseph reveals himself to his brothers. (**14**)
_____Jacob and his family settle in Goshen. (**16**)
_____Joseph interprets the cow dream for Pharaoh who appoints him ruler over Egypt, second only to Pharaoh himself. (**7**)
_____Ten of Joseph's brothers go to Egypt to buy grain at Jacob's request. (**9**)
_____While in prison, Joseph interprets the dreams of the baker and the butler. (**6**)

**WRITTEN FOR OUR LEARNING**

# BRING IT HOME:

**(SCHOLAR & SCRIBE)** Romans 8:28 tells us that all things work together for good to those who love God and are called according to His purpose. Ask your parents about a specific "thing" in their lives that happened because of God's providence.

---

# ➜ BEYOND THE LESSON:

**(SCHOLAR & SCRIBE)** Today people have different ways to show they're very sad or express their grief. Read Genesis 37:29, 37:34, and 44:13. In each verse, identify who is very sad (or upset), why that person(s) is/are sad, and what he/they do to show his/their grief?

Answer: Genesis 37:29—**Reuben, because Joseph is not in the pit and possibly dead, tore his clothes**; Genesis 37:34—**Jacob, because he believes Joseph is dead, tore his clothes**; Genesis 44:13—**Joseph's brothers, because they discover a silver cup in Benjamin's sack, tore their clothes**

**(SCHOLAR)** Read Genesis 45:18 about Pharaoh's instructions concerning the arrival of Joseph's family from Canaan. A common phrase we hear people say today is found at the end of this verse. What does "fat of the land" mean?

Answer: **The best or the richest part of anything; living well by being fed by abundant crops**

**(SCRIBE)** The Bible records several instances where Joseph weeps or cries. Three of those are found in Genesis 42:24, 43:30, and 50:17. Which of those three verses tells us that Joseph has to leave the room to do so and why?

## JOSEPH: BLESSINGS THROUGH GOD'S PROVIDENCE

## - LESSON 6 -
# MOSES: EXCUSES, EXCUSES, EXCUSES!

Scripture Text: Exodus 1; 2:23-25; 3; 4:1-17

 ## BEFORE THE EVENT:

Joseph's family has a new home in Goshen in the land of Egypt. The 12 sons of Israel die, and their children represent the fifth generation to be born after God's covenant with Abraham. The Israelites, as they are now known, are "fruitful and increased abundantly, multiplied and grew exceedingly mighty; and the land was filled with them" (Exodus 1:7). Abraham's descendants have now grown into their own nation called Israel.

- Joseph's Promise to Jacob (Genesis 47:27-31): As the end of his life draws near, Jacob tells Joseph not to bury him in Egypt and instead to bury him with Abraham and Isaac.
- Jacob's Blessings and Last Words for His Sons (Genesis 48–49): Israel speaks to his sons shortly before his death.
- Jacob's Blessings for Manasseh and Ephraim (Genesis 48:12-20): Although Isaac unwittingly had given Jacob the blessings that rightfully belonged to Esau the firstborn, Jacob intentionally blesses Joseph's younger son Ephraim, placing him above his older brother Manasseh.
- Jacob's Death (Genesis 49:29-33; Genesis 50:1-12): Jacob is 147 years old when he dies and his sons bury him in the cave in the field of Machpelah before Mamre in the land of Canaan, the resting place of Abraham, Sarah, Isaac, Rebekah, and Jacob's first wife Leah.
- Joseph's Death (Genesis 50:22-26): Before Joseph dies at age 110, he reassures his family that God will bring them out of Egypt to the land God promised to Abraham, Isaac, and Jacob.

 ## LESSON:

You've probably heard of Moses. Like Joseph, the Bible tells us a lot about Moses. And, like Joseph, Moses is a major figure in the history of God's people and in the fulfillment of God's covenant with Abraham.

Time-wise, it's been about 350 years since Jacob moved his family from Canaan to Goshen in Egypt where Joseph reigned as governor of the

 ## BIBLE WORD OF THE DAY:

ELOQUENT

Definition: Having expressive speech (Exodus 4:10).

"Now a certain Jew named Apollos, born at Alexandria, an **eloquent** man and mighty in the Scriptures, came to Ephesus" (Acts 18:24).

## BIBLE VERSES

Exodus 1:8-10
Exodus 2:23-25
Exodus 3:9-10
Exodus 3:11
Exodus 4:10

 ## BIG IDEA

(SCHOLAR & SCRIBE) Through faith we are confident that God provides everything we need to work in His kingdom.

land. During that time, Abraham's descendants increase dramatically in number, so much so that they become a nation. Unfortunately, there's a new Pharaoh in town.

## (READ EXODUS 1:8-10)

**BRING IT UP**

**(SCHOLAR & SCRIBE)** What are some excuses Christians use in order to avoid working in the church today?

Feeling threatened by the Israelites in his land, the Pharaoh forces them into slavery, giving power to taskmasters to be harsh in dealing with them. Pharaoh wants to make their lives miserable to prevent them from becoming too powerful. However, the harsh treatment backfires: The Israelites continue to flourish and multiply in numbers. So, the Pharaoh implements a more direct ploy to get rid of the Israelites. That is, to kill the all the male children born to Hebrew women. First he orders two Hebrew midwives to kill them right after birth, but the women fear God and refuse to submit to Pharaoh's evil order. Pharaoh then orders his people to kill all of the male babies to be thrown into the Nile River.

It's in that same river that a Levite couple place their infant son in a makeshift basket of bulrushes and set it afloat among the reeds—an excellent hiding place from the Egyptian authorities. But not from Pharaoh's daughter, who sees the ark as she goes to the river to bathe. Long story short, this infant named Moses becomes her son, an Israelite who will be raised in a royal Egyptian family. Even though he grows up surrounded by luxury and privilege, Moses does not forget his family roots.

The Israelites continue to live in bondage at the hands of the Egyptians, and by this time they have been "strangers in a foreign land" more than 400 years.

## (READ EXODUS 2:23-25)

It's a typical day for Moses, tending his father-in-law's flock of sheep when the angel of the Lord appears to him in a flame of fire from a bush. It is a magnificent sight because the bush is burning but is not burning up—so he naturally wonders why the bush is not being burned. Then from the bush God calls Moses and tells him to take off his sandals because he's standing on holy ground. God identifies Himself as the "God of your father—the God of Abraham, the God of Isaac, and the God of Jacob" (Exodus 3:6). God tells Moses it is time for His people to leave Egypt for Canaan, the land He promised Abraham in His covenant.

## (READ EXODUS 3:9-10)

However, Moses isn't eager to take the job. In fact, what immediately comes out of Moses' mouth is a string of excuses.

## (READ EXODUS 3:11)

God assures Moses that He will be with him when he deals with both Pharaoh and the children of Israel, providing signs and wonders to demonstrate that God is I AM WHO I AM (Exodus 3:14). God shows Moses how his rod, when thrown to the ground, miraculously becomes a serpent, and when Moses grabs the serpent by its tail, it becomes a rod again. He then shows Moses a second sign in which Moses' hand becomes leprous when he puts it in his bosom. When he puts his leprous hand back in his

**WRITTEN FOR OUR LEARNING**

cloak, his flesh is restored back to normal. The Lord then tells Moses that the third sign is that He will turn the water from the Nile River into blood. So has God convinced Moses that he should lead His people out of Egypt?

No. And Moses offers another excuse.

## (READ EXODUS 4:10)

God's response? He will be Moses' mouth, guiding him what to say. Then Moses flat-out tells God to get someone else to do it. At this, the Bible says, "The anger of the Lord was kindled against Moses" (Exodus 4:13). Yet, God doesn't give up on Moses, telling Moses that his older brother Aaron is an excellent speaker and will serve as Moses' spokesman to the people. And God doesn't give up on us when we make excuses to avoid working for Him today. Like Moses, we need faith in God that He is with us, and as our faith grows our excuses disappear.

---

## BIBLE BASICS:

1. Where are the children of Israel at the beginning of Exodus? **Egypt**
2. Why does Pharaoh put the Israelites in Egyptian bondage? **Because he's afraid the Israelites are growing too much in number and in strength**
3. When treating the Israelites more harshly didn't work, what does Pharaoh command two Hebrew midwives to do? **Kill the male Hebrew babies at birth**
4. When the Hebrew midwives refuse to obey Pharaoh, what is Pharaoh's command regarding the male babies? **To throw them into the Nile River**
5. Moses is from what tribe or a descendant of what son of Israel? **Levi**
6. Who finds the baby Moses in the basket by the river reeds? **Pharaoh's daughter**
7. From what does the Lord appear to Moses? **A burning bush**
8. What is unusual about the burning bush? **It burns but the bush is not burned or consumed**
9. What does God tell Moses to take off because he's on holy ground? **His sandals**
10. What does God tell Moses to do regarding the Israelites? **To lead them out of Egypt and to the land that He promised in the covenant He made with Abraham**
11. What does Moses say that causes the anger of the Lord to be kindled? **He tells God to send someone else to lead the people**
12. Who does God select to be Moses' spokesman? **His brother Aaron**

---

## BESIDE THE POINT:

**(SCHOLAR)** Compare Exodus 1:8-22 and Matthew 2:1-6, 13-18. Why are male babies being killed in each passage? In Matthew 2:13-14, where does God tell Joseph to take his family because Herod seeks to kill the baby Jesus?

**MOSES: EXCUSES, EXCUSES, EXCUSES!**

Answer: 1a) The Egyptian Pharaoh feels threatened by the growing Israelite population and orders taskmasters "to afflict them with their burdens" (vs. 11) and to make "their lives bitter with hard bondage" (vs. 13). Then Pharaoh tries to force two God-fearing Hebrew midwives, Shiphrah and Puah, to kill the male Israelite babies at birth, but the women refuse to do this. As a result, God blesses these women, and the Israelite people continue to multiply and grow very mighty (vs. 20). The Pharaoh then orders that every male baby born be thrown into the Nile River in order to stop the growth of God's people.

1b) King Herod is "troubled" (vs. 3) when he learns that the King of the Jews has been born. After gathering the chief priests and scribes, he discovers that the Christ is to be born in Bethlehem according to Micah 5:2. Herod's first plan is to order the wise men to search for this baby, and when they find Him, let him know so he can come to worship Him (vs. 8). The wise men don't return, so Herod figures out they outsmarted him, making him "exceedingly angry" (vs. 16). His next plan is more drastic: ordering the mass murder of all male children two years old and under in Bethlehem, where the baby Jesus was born.

2) An angel of the Lord directs Joseph in a dream to take Mary and the baby Jesus to flee to Egypt because King Herod seeks to destroy Him. They remain in Egypt until the death of Herod. (vs. 15 is the fulfillment of the prophet Hosea, in Hosea 11:1: "When Israel was a child, I loved him, and out of Egypt, I called My Son.")

**(SCRIBE)** Throughout the Old Testament, we find individuals with names that have significant meanings pertaining to the circumstances in which we read about them. Remember in Lesson 1 the name Isaac means "laughter," a reminder that both his parents laughed at the idea of becoming parents as such an old age. Consider the names of the following men we've studied so far and the meanings of their names. Using the Scripture references, why were they given these particular names?

- ✛ Abraham: Father of a multitude (Genesis 17:4-6)
- ✛ Esau: Hairy (Genesis 25:25)
- ✛ Jacob: Heel-holder (Genesis 25:26)
- ✛ Israel: God contended (Genesis 32:28)
- ✛ Reuben: Behold, a son (Genesis 29:31-32)
- ✛ Judah: Praise the Lord (Genesis 29:35, Matthew 1:3—Jesus' ancestor)
- ✛ Joseph: He will add (Genesis 30:22-24)
- ✛ Ben-Oni: Son of my sorrow (Genesis 35:16-18)
- ✛ Benjamin: Son of the right hand (Genesis 35:18)
- ✛ Moses: He who draws out (Exodus 2:10)

---

# BRING IT HOME:

**(SCHOLAR & SCRIBE)** As we discussed in Lesson 1, the Israelites knew about their kinfolk as family history and genealogy were important to them. And in this lesson, we looked at the origin and meaning of the names of a few men early in Israel's history. Perhaps your own name has an interesting story behind it. Ask your parents how they decided your first and/or middle name. Are you named after another family member, or was your name chosen to honor a friend? What is the origin of your last name (and your mother's last name if you carry your father's last name)? If your parents don't know, suggest that you and parents conduct a little online research, particularly visiting genealogy websites.

## ➡ BEYOND THE LESSON:

**(SCHOLAR & SCRIBE)** Moses is not the only one in the Bible who makes excuses to God. Read Jeremiah 1:4-8. When God calls Jeremiah to be a prophet for His people, what is Jeremiah's excuse and God's answer?

Answer: **"…Behold I cannot speak, for I am a youth" (vs. 6); "Do not be afraid of their faces, for I am with you to deliver you" (vs. 8)**

**(SCRIBE)** Read Genesis 15:13-14 where God speaks to Abraham concerning His covenant. Where will Abraham's descendants be strangers and about how many years will they be afflicted there?

Answer: **In a land that is not theirs (Egypt); 400 years**

**WRITTEN FOR OUR LEARNING**

# - LESSON 7 -

# AARON: A GOLDEN MISTAKE BY FOLLOWING THE HERD

Scripture Text: Exodus 24:1-12, 32

## BEFORE THE EVENT:

After Moses overcomes his reluctance, he pays a visit to Pharaoh, telling the Egyptian king, "Thus says the Lord God of Israel, 'Let My people go!'" Pharaoh doesn't. So God gives a discouraged Moses another pep talk, assuring him that He remembers His covenant with Abraham and will be with Moses as he leads the Israelites out of Egypt. Pharaoh's heart continues to be hardened, refusing to allow God's people go.

- The First 9 of 10 Plagues (Exodus 7—10): After the miraculous signs and wonders fail to impress Pharaoh enough to let God's people go, God sends destructive plagues upon the land of Egypt.
- The 10th Plague (Exodus 12:29-30): An angel of God kills the firstborn in all of the houses in Egypt, causing great anguish in the land, but spares those in the houses of Israel.
- Pharaoh Finally Lets God's People Go (Exodus 12:31-42): After some 430 years, the children of Israel leave Egypt.
- Red Sea Crossing (Exodus 14): When Moses stretches out his hand over the sea, God provides a dry path for the Israelites and then provides a watery grave for the pursuing Egyptians.
- Mount Sinai Arrival (Exodus 19): Three months after departing Egypt, the Israelites arrive at Mount Sinai, where Moses receives the 10 Commandments, as well as specific instructions governing the construction of the tabernacle.

## LESSON:

Under the leadership of Moses and with the guidance of God, the Israelites flee Egypt, leaving behind many sad and difficult years as slaves. Now they can look forward to a better life in the land God promised to their father Abraham. Three months after this exodus, the children of Israel arrive at the Wilderness of Sinai where they set up camp for a while. Perhaps you've heard of Mount Sinai, where Moses receives the Ten Commandments from God. God also gives Moses numerous laws to govern them in daily life, as well as detailed instructions on how to build the tabernacle.

## BIBLE WORD OF THE DAY:

CORRUPTED

Definition: To ruin, spoil, or destroy (Exodus 32:7).

"*So God looked upon the earth, and indeed it was **corrupt**; for all flesh had corrupted their way on the earth*" (Genesis 6:12).

## BIBLE VERSES

Exodus 24:9, 12
Exodus 24:14-15
Exodus 32:1
Exodus 32:7-10
Exodus 32:19-20

## BIG IDEA

**(SCHOLAR)** Taking responsibility instead of placing blame on others for your actions leads to spiritual growth.

*(continued on next page...)*

But before this, God invites a few people to approach Him, although only Moses will be allowed to go near Him at the top of the mountain.

## (READ EXODUS 24:9, 12)

As Moses and his assistant Joshua head up the mountain, Moses tells the elders to wait for him.

## (READ EXODUS 24:14-15)

Basically, Moses tells the elders to wait for him and puts Aaron in charge if the people have a problem. Unfortunately, the people get tired of waiting. And that's a problem.

## (READ EXODUS 32:1)

Moses is with God 40 days. But the impatient Israelites approach his brother at some point before then, concluding that "this Moses" is not going to come back to them at all. In their minds, the sensible thing to do is for Aaron to make a false god for them to follow and worship. Aaron is Moses' trusted brother selected by God to be a spokesman for Moses. Aaron is among those who just days earlier was in the very presence of God Himself. And so, Aaron is in charge because Moses knows he will make decisions acceptable and in accordance to God's will.

Apparently not. Aaron goes along with their request, which marks the beginning of numerous occasions when the Israelites turn away from God and to false gods because of their lack of faith and memory of His covenant with Abraham. Collecting golden earrings from the people, Aaron crafts a golden calf which they praise for bringing them out of Egypt. He then builds an altar for the idol and proclaims the next day as a feast day to the Lord complete with burnt and peace offerings for sacrifices, food and drink for the people, and other unholy acts of worship for their own pleasure.

Meanwhile, on the mountain…God updates Moses on what's going on down there.

## (READ EXODUS 32:7-10)

Moses pleads with God on Israel's behalf, asking Him to spare their lives and to remember the covenant He made with Abraham. God decides not to destroy them for this wickedness. Moses then comes down the mountain. In his hands are the two tablets bearing the Ten Commandments, written with the finger of God. Moses continues his descent when he sees his assistant Joshua and the two discuss the shouting they hear from the people's camp.

## (READ EXODUS 32:19-20)

Then Moses confronts his brother about how this great sin against God could have happened. Aaron offers up a feeble excuse, blaming the people and their evil tendencies. Instead of admitting he actually made the golden idol, he tells Moses that the people gave him broken pieces of gold and "I cast it into

---

**(SCRIBE)** Following the crowd instead of following God is never the right decision.

## BRING IT UP

**(SCHOLAR & SCRIBE)** Why do you think Aaron goes along with the people's request to build the golden calf?

**(SCHOLAR & SCRIBE)** What can we learn by Aaron's example regarding his decision to make the golden calf and his excuse to Moses about it?

the fire, and this calf came out" (vs. 25). To remove this terrible sin from their lives, Moses intercedes and asks God to forgive them. God then instructs Moses to "lead the people to the place of which I have spoken to you. Behold, My Angel shall go before you" (vs. 34). However, this sin does not go unpunished, and as we will read in future lessons, the Israelites will be punished or plagued by God because of the recurrence of this sin of idolatry.

## BIBLE BASICS:

1. Along with 70 of the elders of Israel, which three men are listed as having seen God? **Aaron, Nadab, and Abihu**
2. Who is with God on Mount Sinai receiving the Ten Commandments and other laws for the Israelites? **Moses**
3. Why do the people tell Aaron to make "gods that shall go before us?" **Because Moses had not returned from the mountain**
4. What does Aaron use to make the golden calf? **Golden earrings**
5. Who tells Moses about the golden calf? **God**
6. While worshiping the false god Aaron made, the Israelites claim that who brought them out of Egypt? **The golden calf**
7. Who pleads with God when God says he will destroy this "stiff-necked people" because they "have corrupted themselves" and have turned away from Him? **Moses**
8. What is Moses carrying when he comes down the mountain? **Two tablets**
9. Who tells Moses he thinks the people are making "a noise of war?" **Joshua**
10. What does Moses do because of his anger against the Israelites worshiping the calf? **Throw down the tablets**
11. Who does Aaron blame for all of this when Moses confronts him? **He blames "the people" who are set on evil**
12. What does God do to them? **He plagues or punishes them**

## BESIDE THE POINT:

**(SCHOLAR)** Read Exodus 32:15-21 about Moses' anger and subsequent reaction regarding the golden calf and the Israelites' idolatrous worship. Then read Matthew 21:12-13 about Jesus' anger toward the moneychangers and His reaction. Compare the two, specifically why Moses and Jesus were angry and discuss in class the appropriateness of anger. Also bring up when anger can get out of hand and become a sin.

**(SCHOLAR & SCRIBE)** It's ironic that while Moses receives the tablets with the Ten Commandment from God, Aaron and the Israelites break the first three of them. What are the first three commandments and how did they break them? (Exodus 20:1-7).

**(SCRIBE)** ) In Exodus 32, we read how the Israelites turn away from God to worship a golden calf. Several times, in this chapter the Bible refers to them as only "the people." There is no capitalization or identification as to whose people they are. Most of the time the Israelites, descendants of Abraham, with whom God made His covenant in Genesis 12, are known by many names throughout the Bible besides the Israelites: Your people and God's chosen people (1 Kings 3:8), for example. Answer the questions below to look at a few more:

1. This name first appears in Genesis 14:13 and describes the man through whom the Israelites descended. **Hebrew**
2. In Exodus 1:9, this name describes the family as becoming numerous and strong. **Children of Israel**
3. Moses writes in Deuteronomy 6:4 that God commands who to "love God with all your heart?" **Israel**
4. The book of James is written to whom (James 1:1)? **The twelve tribes (which are scattered abroad)**
5. This name first appears in Esther 2:5 to describe Esther's cousin Mordecai. **Jew**
6. In Ezra 6:7, King Darius orders for this group to resume work on the temple. **Jews**
7. Zechariah 9:9 uses these two names to tell the Israelites to rejoice because of the coming of the Messiah. **Daughter of Zion, Daughter of Jerusalem**

##  BRING IT HOME:

**(SCHOLAR & SCRIBE)** With your parents or other family members, use your Bible concordance to locate the other Scripture passage that contains the Ten Commandments (**Deuteronomy 5:1-22**). Discuss each commandment and determine which one is not a commandment in the New Testament (**Remember the Sabbath day and keep it holy**).

##  BEYOND THE LESSON:

**(SCHOLAR)** Read Leviticus 10:1-2. What happens to Aaron's sons Nadab and Abihu who also see God (Exodus 24:9-10) but later offer a unauthorized fire to God?

Answer: **The fire devoured them and they died before the Lord**

**(SCHOLAR & SCRIBE)** Moses smashes the two tablets with the Ten Commandments in anger over the people's sinful behavior. Is there another set of tablets?

Answer: **Yes (Deuteronomy 10:1-2). Later on these tablets are kept in the Ark of the Covenant**

**(SCRIBE)** Aaron blames the Israelites for his decision to make the golden calf. Read Genesis 3:11-12 when God asks Adam about eating the forbidden fruit. Who does Adam blame for his decision to eat it?

Answer: **Eve**

**WRITTEN FOR OUR LEARNING**

# - LESSON 8 -
# RAHAB: SALVATION WHEN THE WALLS COME TUMBLING DOWN

Scripture Text: Joshua 2–6

## BEFORE THE EVENT:

Two new tablets of stone for the Ten Commandments replace the ones Moses broke in the last lesson. When he comes down the mountain this time with the tablets, Moses' face shines, causing the people to be afraid of him. Moses puts in motion all of the laws to be a guide for the people in their daily lives. The tabernacle, Israel's center of worship, is built.

+ Faithless in the Wilderness (Deuteronomy 1): In spite of all God has done for them, the Israelites rebel and refuse to go further toward Canaan because of their lack of faith in Him.
+ Spies in Canaan (Numbers 13): Moses sends 12 spies to investigate the land of Canaan, and Caleb speaks out against the 10 men's negative reports.
+ Israel Punished (Numbers 14; Deuteronomy 1:34-46): Because of their rebellion and lack of faith, "this evil generation" of those 20 and older die in the wilderness and are not allowed into the Promised Land; Caleb and Joshua are the exceptions.
+ Moses Sees the Promised Land (Deuteronomy 34:1-4): Because of Moses' sin (striking the rock at Meribah, Numbers 20), the Lord does not allow Moses to lead the people into Canaan but does allow him to see it from afar from Mount Nebo.
+ Moses Dies (Deuteronomy 34:5-8): The servant of the Lord dies at 120 years of age and is buried by God in the land of Moab.
+ Joshua Begins to Lead (Joshua 1:1-9): Joshua takes over to lead the Israelites into Canaan.

## LESSON:

It's been 40 years since the Israelites escaped Egyptian bondage, and for most of that time, they have been wandering in the wilderness not too far from their ultimate destination: The land of Canaan, which God promised to Abraham and his descendants more than 600 years earlier. During these 40 years, the Israelites grow increasingly impatient and dissatisfied, causing them to angrily complain time and time again—a direct result of their lack of faith in God. So, God does not allow these

## BIBLE WORD OF THE DAY:

FAINTHEARTED

Definition: Fearful; lacking courage (Joshua 2:9).

"...For indeed all inhabitants of the country are **fainthearted** because of us" (Joshua 2:24).

## BIBLE VERSES
Joshua 2:4-5
Joshua 2:9-10
Joshua 2:12-14
Joshua 2:17

## BIG IDEA
(SCHOLAR & SCRIBE) Let your faith in God be the first thing others see in you.

faithless complainers to enter the Promised Land.

However, today we will look at a woman who, by her words and her actions, shows a great unwavering faith in God. Funny thing is, she's not an Israelite. In fact, she's a Canaanite from a country steeped in the pagan worship of false gods. Her name is Rahab. And you'll find her name not only in the early chapters of Joshua but also in the New Testament books of Hebrews and James, which hold her up as a fine example of faith, and in Matthew which lists her as an ancestor in Jesus' family tree. This lowly woman, a prostitute, from a pagan country plays a key role in both God's covenant with Abraham and God's plan of salvation.

Joshua, Moses' successor to lead the children of Israel into Canaan, prepares to conquer the main city of Jericho by sending out spies to see what he's up against. The spies come to Rahab's house and stay there. Word gets out Israelite spies are in town, and the king of Jericho has reason to believe these spies are in Rahab's house. The king's officers knock on Rahab's door telling her to bring the spies out.

## BRING IT UP

**(SCHOLAR & SCRIBE)** The memorial of 12 stones commemorates the Lord's miracle of stopping the waters of the Jordan River in order that His people could cross over (Exodus 4). What is the purpose of memorials in general? What are some memorials you have visited or memorials you would like to visit someday?

### (READ JOSHUA 2:4-5)

After convincing them the spies are long gone and have disappeared into the dark night, Rahab sends the king's men on a wild goose chase all the way to the Jordan River when she knows good and well the spies are safely tucked away on her roof, hiding by stalks of flax, which by the way is a type of fiber to make clothes. (We know that it's wrong to lie, but Rahab is doing her best to save the men sent by Joshua.) Before the spies go to sleep, Rahab goes up to the roof to speak to them.

### (READ JOSHUA 2:9-10)

Simply put, the people of Jericho are scared to death of the Israelites. God has delivered the Israelites in many ways, and Rahab recounts just two of them. Because of its reputation, Israel is a nation to be feared among other countries, Canaan included. This is valuable information for the spies to hear and later report to Joshua. Rahab says that Israel's God is "God of heaven above and on earth beneath" and knows that He has given this land to them. This same faith in the one true God gives Rahab the strength to risk her life by saving the Israelites spies. She also has faith that the spies can save her and her family.

### (READ JOSHUA 2:12-14)

They have a deal. Because Rahab's house is situated within the city wall that surrounds Jericho, the spies instruct her to hang a scarlet cord in her window so they will know where she and her family are when the Israelites attack Jericho. The spies assure her that every member of her household in her home at that time will be saved when Jericho is destroyed. Rahab agrees to hang the scarlet cord in her window as a sign to them. When the spies return to Joshua, they report that the Lord has delivered Canaan into their hands because inhabitants of the land are fainthearted because of them, just as Rahab had told them.

God gives Joshua instructions for taking the city of Jericho: March around the city once for six days with seven priests bearing seven trumpets of rams' horns before the Ark of the Covenant. On the seventh day, march around the city seven times and the priests will blow their trumpets. At the sound of a long blast with the ram's horn and the sound of the trumpet, all the people shall shout a great shout. Then the wall of Jericho will fall down flat.

### (READ JOSHUA 2:17)

## BIBLE BASICS:

1. Who sends two spies to view the land of Jericho? **Joshua**
2. Where do the spies hide? **Rahab's house**
3. Where is Rahab's house? **Within the city wall surrounding Jericho**
4. Where specifically in Rahab's house are the spies hiding? **On the roof under the stalks of flax**
5. What two events does Rahab tell the spies that cause the inhabitants of Jericho to be afraid of the Israelites? **Israelites crossing the Red Sea, and Israelites utterly destroying the two Amorite kings, Sihon and Og**
6. What does Rahab, a Canaanite, think about Israel's God? **"The Lord your God, He is God in heaven above and on earth beneath" (2:11).**
7. Because she is kind to the spies, protecting them from the king of Jericho by hiding them, what does she ask the spies in return? **That they spare her and her family's life when Israel invades Jericho**
8. What do the spies tell Rahab to do to ensure her family is saved from the destruction of Jericho? **To hang a scarlet cord in her window to identify her house and all her family members must be inside her home**
9. What river does Israel cross before reaching Jericho? (3:1-17) **The Jordan**
10. How many stones are gathered for a memorial commemorating the day the waters of the Jordan were cut off before those carrying the Ark of the Covenant crossed over on dry land? **12**
11. What are God's instructions to Joshua on taking Jericho? **March around the city once for six days with seven priests bearing seven trumpets of rams' horns before the Ark of the Covenant. On the seventh day, march around the city seven times and the priests shall blow their trumpets. At the sound of a long blast and the sound of the trumpet, all of the people shall shout a great shout. Then the wall of the city will fall down flat.**
12. What happens to Rahab and her family when Jericho falls? **She and everyone in her household live because she hid the messengers who Joshua sent to spy out Jericho**

## BESIDE THE POINT:

**(SCHOLAR)** Compare Moses and Joshua as men and leaders of the Israelites. How are they similar and how are they different? Below are some examples to get started:
+ Meaning of their names: Moses (To Draw Out); Joshua (The Lord Saves)
+ Tribe: Moses (Levi, Exodus 2:1-10); Joshua (Ephraim, Numbers 13:7—You may want to explain that Joseph's sons, Ephraim and Manasseh, were tribes as there was not a tribe from Joseph.)

## RAHAB: SALVATION WHEN THE WALLS COME TUMBLING DOWN

- Occupation: Moses (Shepherd, Exodus 3:1) Joshua (Moses' Assistant, Exodus 24:13, one of 12 spies on Canaan, Numbers 13)
- Purpose: Moses (Lead the People out of Egypt); Joshua (Lead the People into Canaan)
- Sandals Removed: Moses (In the presence of God at the Burning Bush, Exodus 3:1-6); Joshua (In the presence of The Commander, Joshua 5:13-15)
- Watery Obstacles: Moses (Crossed the Red Sea, Exodus 14); Joshua (Crossed the Jordan River, Joshua 3)
- Interceded to God on Israel's behalf: Moses: (After the golden calf episode [Exodus 32:30-34]); Joshua (After the sin at Ai, Joshua 7:6-9)
- Servant of the Lord: Moses (Joshua 1:1) and Joshua (24:29) called this
- In General: Both Moses and Joshua begin serving as Israel's leader at age 80; Moses lived to 120; Joshua, 110

**(SCRIBE)** Review and compare the Israelites' journey across the Red Sea in Exodus 14 and the Jordan River in Joshua 3. Below are a few comparisons.

- Israelite Leader: The Red Sea, Moses; The Jordan River, Joshua
- A Guide for the Israelites: The Red Sea, Angel of God and Pillar of Cloud (Exodus 14:19); The Jordan River, Ark of the Covenant (Joshua 3:6)
- Signal to Part: The Red Sea, Moses stretches out his hand (Exodus 14:21); The Jordan River, the feet of the priests bearing the Ark of the Covenant touch the water (Joshua 3:14-15)
- Casualties: The Red Sea, Unsuspecting Egyptians pursuing the Israelites (Exodus 14:26-28); The Jordan River, None
- Commemorating the Crossing: The Red Sea, Moses writes and sings a psalm of praise to God (Exodus 15:1-21); The Jordan River, Joshua instructs 12 men to gather 12 stones from the Jordan (one man from each tribe gathers one stone) for a memorial that all may know "the hand of the Lord, that it is mighty, that you may fear the Lord your God forever" (Joshua 4:24).

# BRING IT HOME:

**(SCHOLAR & SCRIBE)** With your parents or other family members, read Ruth 4:18-22 and Matthew 1:1-3. Figure out Rahab's relationship to David. (**She's his great-great grandmother.**)

# ➡ BEYOND THE LESSON:

**(SCHOLAR & SCRIBE)** As we discussed, Rehab is one of four women mentioned by name in Jesus' genealogy in Matthew 1. Tamar is another (Matthew 1:2). Both Rahab and Tamar are from Canaan. Read Genesis 38:27-30. What other thing do the two women have in common?

Answer: **A scarlet cord or thread is wound in the stories of their lives**

**WRITTEN FOR OUR LEARNING**

**(SCHOLAR & SCRIBE)** Read Exodus 17:1-7 and Numbers 20:1-13. In both, the Israelites are angry at Moses because of there's no water—in Exodus shortly after they cross the Red Sea and in Numbers after wandering in the wilderness 40 years later. What does God tell Moses to do in each case? What does Moses do in each case? What punishment does Moses receive as a result of his actions in Numbers?

Answer: **In Exodus: God tells Moses to strike the rock; Moses strikes the rock and water comes out. In Numbers: God tells Moses to take the rod and Aaron and speak to the rock; Moses strikes the rock twice with his rod and water comes out; Moses is not allowed to lead the people into Canaan.**

WRITTEN FOR OUR LEARNING

## - LESSON 9 -

# EHUD: KING EGLON GETS THE POINT

Scripture Text: Judges 3

 ## BEFORE THE EVENT:

Although Jericho quickly collapses into the hands of the Israelites, over time, other nations in the land of Canaan also succumb to Israel. But not all of them. The land that Israel possesses is divided among the 12 tribes and they begin a new life there. God's promise to Abraham to give his descendants the land of Canaan is now a reality. However, before he dies, Joshua warns them that if they transgress the covenant of the Lord by serving other gods, the anger of the Lord will burn against them and they shall perish quickly from the good land that He has given them (Joshua 23:16).

- ✦ Israel's Unfaithfulness (Judges 2:11-13): A new generation of God's people don't know God and turn to false gods.
- ✦ God's Response (Judges 2:14-23): God punishes His people allowing neighboring nations to oppress them and then raises up judges to deliver them from their suffering.
- ✦ Israelites' Intermingling (Judges 3:1-6): The sons and daughters of God's people marry those from pagan nations and adopt their idolatrous ways.
- ✦ Othniel (Judges 3:7-11): The first judge who God raises is Othniel, the nephew of Caleb, one of the 12 spies sent out by Moses to view the land of Canaan.

 ## LESSON:

The topic for this week's lesson is every student's favorite: Punishment. Or sometimes we use the word discipline. For example, you disobey your parents at home and you are punished. Or, you don't follow the teacher's instructions at school and you are disciplined. Punishment is a way for you to "learn your lesson" and not do whatever it was that got you in trouble again. Punishment comes in a variety of forms designed to change the behavior that warranted the punishment in the first place. For recurring misbehavior or for especially bad behavior, the punishment is often harsh or severe.

Such is the case for the badly misbehaving Israelites as they settle in Canaan, the land God promised them in His covenant with Abraham.

## BIBLE WORD OF THE DAY:

EVIL

Definition: Morally wrong, sinful, or wicked (Judges 3:7).

*"So the Lord's anger was aroused against Israel, and He made them wander in the wilderness forty years, until all the generation that had done **evil** in the sight of the Lord was gone"*
(Numbers 32:13).

## BIBLE VERSES

Judges 3:7
Judges 3:12
Judges 3:13-14
Judges 3:21-22

## BIG IDEA

**(SCHOLAR)** God does not allow sin to go unpunished.

*(continued on next page...)*

Unfortunately, the children of Israel seem to be plagued with both short- and long-term memory loss. They forget all that God has done for them, the miracles He has performed on their behalf, and the promises He has kept because of His covenant.

## (READ JUDGES 3:7)

These are two of the many false gods the arrogant and wayward Israelites choose to worship. The people don't care that this is a flagrant sin against God. So how do you think God reacts to His people turning to these pagan idols and away from Him? The Bible says the Lord's anger is "hot against Israel." Because the Lord loves the Israelites, He does not want them to continue in this sin and decides to punish them. This wicked sin of their betrayal of God and misplaced loyalty to gods that don't even exist is so horrible that God punishes them by allowing surrounding pagan nations to dominate and oppress the Israelites that will cause great suffering among His people. In this instance, they are sold as slaves to the king of Mesopotamia. After eight years living in miserable conditions under an enemy's rule, the Israelites cry out to the Lord for help, to rescue them from their suffering. He does so by raising up a leader called a judge, who defeats the Mesopotamian king. The nation of Israel is restored and His people are faithful and worship the Lord again. However, this period of rest and peace among the Israelites is short-lived, lasting only 40 years. Because when Othniel dies…

**(SCRIBE)** God punishes the Israelites for their wickedness by allowing wicked nations to oppress them.

## BRING IT UP

**(SCHOLAR)** Why do you think this event includes many details and graphic descriptions?

**(SCRIBE)** Why do you think God allows Moab to rule over the Israelites for so long?

## (READ JUDGES 3:12)

Apparently, the Israelites have not learned their lesson. So, God must punish them again.

## (READ JUDGES 3:13-14)

After those 18 years, the children of Israel again cry out to the Lord and again the Lord raises up the judge Ehud to deliver the repentant people from Eglon the king of Moab. The Bible gives us many details on what happens between Ehud and Eglon. Ehud is from the tribe of Benjamin, and the Bible tells us he's left-handed. That may not seem like an important detail, but you'll see in a moment why it is. Being left-handed is unusual both then and today, as only ten percent of the population is left-handed. Ehud pays a visit to King Eglon at his palace. The reason for his visit is to pay Israel's tribute (money owed to the king from nations under his rule) to Eglon. It's also important to note that Eglon was a very fat man. Anyway, Ehud prepares for this meeting by making a double-edged dagger about 18 inches long, not very big. He packs it under his clothes, fastening it on his right thigh. If Ehud were right-handed, he would've attached the sword to his left thigh. Because he's left-handed, the guards would not have seen his weapon hidden on his right thigh. They would have checked his left thigh for a weapon assuming the judge would be right-handed. So Ehud easily is able to visit the king with his dagger safely tucked on his right thigh.

After paying his tribute, Ehud meets with King Eglon alone upstairs in his private chambers and says he has a message from God for him.

## (READ JUDGES 3:21-22)

Ehud does not hang around for Eglon's gut reaction to all this and quickly exits through the porch, locking and shutting the doors behind him as he makes his escape. Meanwhile, on the other side of the upper chambers, Eglon's guards wait patiently for the king, totally unaware that he has just been killed by his Israelite guest. By the time the guards go inside to check on the king, Ehud is long gone. He blows a ram's horn in the mountains of Ephraim and the children of Israel come down. Ehud announces that the Lord has delivered their enemies the Moabites into their hands. With the power of God behind them, the Israelites battle the people of Moab, killing about 10,000 that day.

## BIBLE BASICS:

1. Why does God not drive out all of the remaining nations in the land? **So that He may test Israel, whether they will keep His ways or not**

2. After Joshua dies, Israel does evil in the sight of the Lord and serves what? **The Baals**

3. Who does God raise up to deliver the people from nations who plunder them? **Judges**

4. In Judges 3:12, the children of Israel do what again in the sight of the Lord? **Evil**

5. Because the children of Israel do evil in the sight of the Lord, whom does God strengthen against them? **King Eglon of Moab**

6. How long does Israel serve King Eglon? **18 years**

7. When does God raise up a deliverer for the children of Israel? **When they cry out to the Lord**

8. What is Ehud's plan to overtake the king? **Ehud visits the king to deliver the tribute owed to him. The left-handed judge hides a small dagger under his clothes fastened on his right thigh. He tells the unsuspecting, obese king that he has a secret message for him, and the two enter the king's private chamber. Alone, Ehud says to Eglon, "I have a message from God for you." And reaching for his sword with his left hand, Ehud thrusts it into Eglon's belly. The fat seems to swallow the sword as even the hilt goes in after the blade. Ehud leaves the dagger in and goes out, locking and shutting the doors of the upper room behind him.**

9. Who finds the dead king? **Eglon's servants who had been waiting for him outside of the chamber**

10. What happens when Ehud blows the trumpet in the mountains of Ephraim? **The children of Israel come down with him from the mountains**

11. How many men from Moab are killed by the Israelites that day? **10,000**

12. After the Moabites are defeated by Israel, the land is at rest for how many years? **80**

## BESIDE THE POINT:

**(SCHOLAR)** Have a class discussion comparing judges in our society today and judges in ancient Israel. Find out what your students think about today's judges by letting them compose a list of their duties on the board. Finetune their thoughts and describe the different types of judges in our country, such as criminal court judges, civil court judges, Supreme Court judges. To summarize, today's judges interpret, uphold,

### EHUD: KING EGLON GETS THE POINT

and enforce our laws. Now look at the judges God appointed and their duties. Read Judges 4:4-5 about Deborah whose duties seem to mirror today's judges. However, her job description changes dramatically in the following verses when she becomes a military leader preparing for a battle. Many of the judges serve in this capacity at one time or another. The Hebrew word for *judge* means "to rule" or "to deliver." The judges also are appointed by God to deliver the Israelites from foreign oppression when they turned back to God. They were also godly rulers who tried to guide an often wayward people bent on following false gods and engaging in all sorts of wickedness and immorality.

**(SCRIBE)** God punishes His people because He loves them and wants them to return to the righteous path of their ancestor Abraham. Similarly, God commands parents to punish or discipline their children to train them in the way they should go (Proverbs 22:6). This is a good time to discuss various punishments your students have endured for certain behaviors. Make sure they understand that their parents discipline them because they love them and want them to be better. If there's time, read these verses on the result of parental punishment: Proverbs 3:12, Proverbs 13:24, and Proverbs 23:13.

# BRING IT HOME:

**(SCHOLAR & SCRIBE)** Ask your parents about the types of punishment and discipline they got when they were growing up. Were they effective in helping them "learn their lesson?" Then ask them why they punish you when you misbehave.

# BEYOND THE LESSON:

**(SCHOLAR)** Ehud is left-handed and descends from the tribe of Benjamin (in which left-handedness is mentioned in Judges 20:16). In that verse, the 700 select, left-handed men come from which tribe?

Answer: **Benjamin**

Read 1 Chronicles 12:2, the only other time the Bible reveals the "handedness" of a person or group of people. In this verse, are these Benjamite warriors providing military aid to David right-handed, left-handed, or ambidextrous (able to use both hands equally)?

Answer: **Ambidextrous**

**(SCRIBE)** King Eglon rules the nation of Moab, where its people worship Baal and other idols. Read Ruth 1:4. Who is also from Moab and marries an Israelite, becoming a direct ancestor of Jesus?

Answer: **Ruth**

## - LESSON 10 -

# SAMSON: A BAD HAIR DAY

Scripture Text: Judges 13–16

 ## BEFORE THE EVENT:

The period of the judges continues after Ehud. When he dies the children of Israel again did evil in the sight of the Lord. (Judges 4:1). Thus begins a series of judges who deliver Israel out of enemies' hands when they turn to idolatry and other wickedness.

- Deborah (Judges 4–5)
- Gideon (Judges 6–8)
- Jephthah (Judges 11)

 ## LESSON:

During the period of the judges, the Israelites' relationship with God is rocky, with good times and bad times. Now Judges 13:1 says, "Again the children of Israel did evil in the sight of the Lord…." This is one of those bad times as the Lord delivers His people into the hand of the Philistines for 40 years. Like He has in the past, God plans to rescue them by sending a judge to lead the way. In this case, God's plan begins even before this judge is born. An angel of the Lord appears to the wife of Manoah, a man from the tribe of Dan, and speaks to her.

### (READ JUDGES 13:5)

This child is born a Nazarite who may not cut his hair and he grows up to be the strongest man in the Bible—Samson. His strength lies in his uncut hair. God raises up Samson to begin to deliver Israel out of the hand of the Philistines. Perhaps you've heard of Samson because Scripture tells us a lot about him, about his God-given strength, and about his relationships with Philistine women. It's that last part that gets Samson in a lot of trouble, the part about being with or marrying women from foreign countries. It's against God's law to marry those from pagan nations, such as Philistia, because of their evil influences to serve other gods (Deuteronomy 7:1-5).

### (READ DEUTERONOMY 7:6)

The Israelites need to be reminded they are a special people, chosen

## BIBLE WORD OF THE DAY:

PILLAR

Definition: A slender, vertical structure or column supporting a building (Judges 16:26).

*"When she looked, there was the king standing by a **pillar** according to custom…"*
(2 Kings 11:14).

## BIBLE VERSES

Judges 13:5
Deuteronomy 7:6
Judges 16:4-5
Judges 16:6-7
Judges 16:17

## BIG IDEA

**(SCHOLAR)** God gives us our strengths, but we make the choice on how to use them.

*(continued on next page...)*

by God Himself. And God has chosen Samson to lead them from the Philistines' evil grasp, but the problem is, Samson is held by the grasp of a particular sneaky, money-hungry Philistine woman named Delilah.

## (READ JUDGES 16:4-5)

That's a lot of money the Philistine lords want to give her for finding out the secret of Samson's strength. These men are willing to pay that much because of the damage Samson and his supernatural strength has already caused their people. As an Israelite, Samson is a real threat to the Philistines, so the lords want to capture Samson and see his love for Delilah as a way to do just that. Delilah apparently loves money more than Samson. She decides to sweet-talk and flatter Samson and lure him into revealing the source of strength so that she can cash in with the Philistine lords. She starts by simply asking Samson, who replies with a simple answer.

## (READ JUDGES 16:6-7)

So, the lords of the Philistines give seven fresh bowstrings not yet dried to Delilah and she binds Samson while the men lie in wait to pounce on him. Delilah then exclaims, "The Philistines are upon you, Samson!" But Samson, who had lied to Delilah about the bowstrings being his secret source of strength, breaks them with no problem. Not amused by his trickery, Delilah asks Samson again. He makes up a story about new ropes that will make him weak as any other man. So, Delilah takes new ropes, binds Samson, and exclaims, "The Philistines are upon you, Samson!" Samson breaks the ropes off his arms as if they were threads. The third time Delilah asks, Samson says if seven locks of his head are woven into the web of the loom, then he will become weak. Again she says, "The Philistines are upon you, Samson!" And again, Samson remains strong.

But his willpower is not so strong. Delilah bugs Samson until he can't take it anymore and finally he tells her the secret.

## (READ JUDGES 16:17)

Delilah realizes that this time, Samson tells her the truth. As the lords lie in wait to attack Samson, Delilah lulls him to sleep on her knees, calls for a man to shave Samson's head, and exclaims, "The Philistines are upon you, Samson!" Samson wakes up, figures he'll shake himself free, but doesn't realize the Lord has left him. So the Philistines capture Samson, put out his eyes, and make him a slave forced to grind grain in prison. His hair, however, begins to grow back.

So, the Philistines hold a big party to offer a great sacrifice to their false god named Dagon. During this celebration, they bring Samson up from prison to perform for them. Holding his hand, a little boy leads the blind Samson who tells him to let him feel the pillars that support the temple. About 3,000 men and women are on the roof watching Samson as he performed. Samson then prays to God for strength, takes hold of the two middle pillars supporting the temple, and pushes with all his might. The temple comes crashing down on all the people in it, including Samson. His family buries Samson with

---

**(SCRIBE)** We must use our God-given strengths for His glory.

## BRING IT UP

**(SCHOLAR)** Considering his faults and weaknesses, why do you think Samson is in the Hebrews 11 list of Old Testament examples of faith?

**(SCRIBE)** Why do you think Samson lies to Delilah three times before telling her the truth about the secret of his strength?

his father Manoah. Samson judged Israel 20 years, and this event is the beginning of the downfall of the Philistines, the conclusion of Samson's purpose when he was called by God.

## BIBLE BASICS:

1. Israel is under the rule of whom? **The Philistines**
2. How many years has Israel been under the rule of the Philistines? **40**
3. Who is Samson's father? **Manoah**
4. From what tribe is Samson? **Dan**
5. What is a Nazarite not to do with his hair? **Cut it**
6. What is the source of Samson's strength? **God and his hair**
7. Who does Samson love from the Valley of Sorek? **Delilah**
8. How much do the lords offer Delilah to find out the source of Samson's strength? **1,100 pieces of silver from each lord**
9. How many times does Samson give Delilah a false answer to her question? **3**
10. After his head is shaved, who leaves Samson? **The Lord**
11. How does Samson become blind? **Philistines put out his eyes**
12. How does Samson die? **By pushing two pillars that support the temple of Dagon, causing it to fall on him and thousands of Philistines**

## BESIDE THE POINT:

**(SCHOLAR)** If you have time, read and discuss the account of Jael and Sisera in Judges 4. Deborah in 4:9 tells Barak that she will go with him and an army from Naphtali and Zebulun to fight Sisera, the commander of Jabin's Canaanite army. She tells Barak that the Lord will sell Sisera into the hand of a woman. That woman ends up being Jael, the wife of Heber the Kenite. Read with your class Judges 4:17-24. Discuss how this event is similar to Ehud's murder of Eglon and how this event is similar to Delilah's manipulation of Samson. Also, look at how God's will for His people prevails in all three events.
**(SCRIBE)** Samson is not the only judge to act on impulse without thinking things through and considering the consequences. Consider the hasty decision of fellow judge Jephthah in Judges 11:29-40. After reading the passage with your class, discuss how to carefully make an important decision that would be pleasing to God.

## BRING IT HOME:

**(SCHOLAR & SCRIBE)** There are so many lessons Christians can learn from the life of Samson. Discuss with your parents about what you've learned this week about Samson. Then ask them what they learned when they studied this Old Testament figure.

### SAMSON: A BAD HAIR DAY

# → BEYOND THE LESSON:

**(SCHOLAR)** There are a few births in the Bible that are divinely pre-announced by an angel of the Lord. Read Judges 13:3-5, Luke 1:11-17, and Luke 1:26-33. Answer the following questions from each passage: Whose birth is announced? To whom is the angel speaking? Why hasn't the mother already given birth to a child? What is the purpose of the child to be born?

Answer: **Samson, Manoah's wife, she is barren, to begin to deliver Israel out of the hand of the Philistines; John the Baptist, Zacharias, she is old, to make ready a people prepared for the Lord; Jesus, Mary, she is a virgin, to reign over the house of Jacob forever and His kingdom will have no end**

**(SCRIBE)** Samson's is one of a few births in the Bible to be divinely pre-announced by an angel of the Lord. Speaking to the wife of Manoah, the angel of the Lord tells her that Samson's purpose is to begin to deliver Israel out of the hand of the Philistines. (Judges 13:3-5) Read Luke 1:26-33. An angel appears to a woman named Mary and tells her she will give birth to a son. What is His name and God's purpose for him?

Answer: **Jesus; He will reign over the house of Jacob forever and His kingdom will have no end**

# - LESSON 11 -

# JOB: JOY THROUGH SUFFERING

Scripture Text: Job

 ## BEFORE THE EVENT:

Bible scholars have not reached a consensus about when the book of Job was written nor when the events therein took place. Contextual clues in the book indicate that it probably took place during the Patriarchal Age, roughly the same time as the events recorded in Genesis and Exodus occurred. By the same token, the writing reflects other books written during the reign of King Solomon several hundred years later. So, while Job does not easily fit chronologically within the lessons in this guide, we chose to place it after the period of the Judges but before the period of the Kings.

 ## LESSON:

At the beginning of the quarter we talked about a man who is described as "blameless." Who remembers him? Abraham! Today, we look at a blameless man who endures horrible tragedies in his life, asks God why He allows such suffering, and in the end learns only God knows the reasons as He knows what is best for his children.

### (READ JOB 1:1-2)

What happens next may seem a bit unusual. God and Satan have a conversation. God tells Satan about Job and how he is a God-fearing man who stays away from evil.

### (READ JOB 1:9)

Basically, Satan argues that it's no wonder Job follows after the Lord only because the Lord has blessed Job to the extent that he's the most prosperous man in the land. Satan wants to see what Job would do if he suddenly doesn't have it so good. He will break down and curse God, Satan says. God allows Satan to do take what Job has but does not allow Satan to lay a hand on Job. In the short span of a day, Satan begins his campaign to take down Job. One right after another, four tragic events occur to try to bring Job to despair and curse God: A group of nomadic raiders steal Job's oxen and donkeys and kill his servants. Then, fire descends from the sky burned and kills Job's sheep and shepherds. Then,

 ## BIBLE WORD OF THE DAY:

ADVERSITY

Definition: Affliction, suffering, hardship, difficulties, etc. (Job 2:11).

*"So nation was destroyed by nation and city by city, for God troubled them with every **adversity**"* (2 Chronicles 15:6).

## BIBLE VERSES

Job 1:1-2
Job 1:9
Job 1:20-22
Job 2:4-5

 ## BIG IDEA

**(SCHOLAR)** Although we may not always understand why bad things happen, God reassures us that these things make us stronger and better in the faith (James 1:2-4).

a group of Chaldeans steals his camels and kills the herders with a sword. In three moments, Job loses his vast wealth and possessions. It gets worse. Satan creates a windstorm that collapses the house where his seven sons and three daughters are having a meal. They are instantly killed.

## (READ JOB 1:20-22)

Does Job curse God and blame Him for these terrible things that happened to him? Instead, Job worships God, acknowledges that he was born with nothing and will die with nothing, and he does not sin. God and Satan talk again. God points out Job passed his test, but Satan wants to kick the suffering up a notch.

## (READ JOB 2:4-5)

God's restriction is that whatever Satan does to Job, Job does not die. God is in control of this whole situation with Job. Satan causes an onslaught of painful boils to ravage his body "from the sole of his foot to the crown of his head." In immense pain and agony, the one-time wealthy man now grieves for his slain children and sits in ashes while he scrapes his sores with a piece of pottery.

**(SCRIBE)** God allows bad things to happen to good people.

## BRING IT UP

**(SCHOLAR)** Why do you think some people want to blame God and turn away from Him during difficult times in their lives?

**(SCRIBE)** How can you be a good friend to someone who is going through a difficult time?

Job's wife apparently witnesses all this but does not give Job helpful advice. She tells her husband to give up, curse God, and die. Job responds to his "foolish" wife by saying that we must praise God in times of prosperity and in times of poverty.

Then Job's three friends—Eliphaz, Bildad, and Zophar—hear about these bad things that happened to Job. They come to mourn and comfort their friend Job. When they first see Job, they don't even recognize him. Then the friends cry with Job, tear their robes, and sprinkle dust on Job's head. They sit down on the ground beside their grieving friend, and no one says anything for seven days. So far Eliphaz, Bildad, and Zophar seem to be pretty good friends to Job. A lot more supportive than his wife—until one of them opens his mouth.

Before Eliphaz tells his friend what he thinks about all this, Job speaks of his sorrow and misery, wishing that he'd never been born. He doesn't curse those who took his possession nor does he curse God, but wants God to let him die.

Instead of being a comforting friend, Eliphaz explains to Job why he is suffering so much. It's because God blesses righteous people and punishes wicked people, Eliphaz mistakenly tells Job. Later, his friend Bildad adds that his sons must have sinned, causing their own deaths as punishment (Job 8:3-4). Zophar urges Job to repent as God really hasn't punished him enough for his sins (Job 11:6). The so-called friends don't let up and continue with their harsh words.

Although Job refuses to blame God for his suffering, he does want to know why these bad things happened. Specifically, why him? From a whirlwind, God answers Job's questions, and first of all, makes it clear to Job who God is, which is humbling to Job to say the least. The question of why God lets good people suffer is not Job's to answer as Job cannot understand how God in His wisdom uses suffering to help the sufferer.

In the end, Job does repent. He's sorry for accusing God of being unfair and for his own self-righteousness. God scolds the three friends for their lies, and Job prays for them. God restores everything Job lost by giving him twice as much as he had before, as well as seven sons and three daughters. God blesses the latter days of Job more than his beginning.

## BIBLE BASICS:

1. Who lives in the land of Uz? **Job**
2. How many children does Job have in the beginning? **10**
3. What is God's restriction on Satan the first time? **Not to lay a hand on Job**
4. What burns because of the fire from the sky? **Job's sheep and shepherds**
5. Who steals Job's camels and kills the herders with a sword? **Chaldeans**
6. What is God's restriction on Satan the second time? **Not to kill Job**
7. What affliction does Satan cast upon Job? **Painful boils**
8. Eliphaz tells Job that God is punishing Job because of what? **Sin**
9. What advice does Job's wife give Job? **Curse God and die**
10. How many of Job's friends give him moral "support?" **Three**
11. What do the friends sprinkle on Job's head? **Dust**
12. What does Job repent of? **Accusing God of unfairness and his own self-righteousness**

## BESIDE THE POINT:

**(SCHOLAR)** In Job 19:25, the Job states that he knows that his Redeemer lives and He shall stand at last on the earth. Read Hebrews 4:15 and 1 Timothy 2:5. What are some ways Jesus suffered while He was on the earth? As a class, make a list of specific difficulties and hardships Jesus endured and compare them with specific suffering Job endured. Then discuss how Jesus, as our Redeemer and Mediator, understands our own suffering during difficult times.

**(SCRIBE)** Many common phrases we hear in everyday conversation originate in the book of Job. Look up and read the following verses and see if you can figure out the phrase or saying found within each.

+ Job 1:21......................**The Lord gives and the Lord takes away**
+ Job 4:8........................**You reap what you sow**
+ Job 19:20....................**By the skin of my teeth**
+ Job 19:28....................**The root of the matter**
+ Job 19:19-20...............**Nothing but skin and bones**
+ Job 31:6......................**Weighed in the balance**
+ Job 40:15....................**Behemoth**

**JOB: JOY THROUGH SUFFERING**

 # BRING IT HOME:

**(SCHOLAR & SCRIBE)** ) This is a good lesson to discuss with your parents and other family members. They probably can share from personal experience how suffering in their lives have helped them grow as Christians. Read James 1:2-3 together as a family and discuss how although we may not understand suffering at the time, we can look back after the experience and see how it made us better individuals.

---

# BEYOND THE LESSON:

**(SCHOLAR)** Read Zechariah 3:1-2 where the prophet has a vision involving Joshua the high priest (not Joshua who succeeded Moses as leader of the Israelites). Who is making accusations against the high priest and God's people?

Answer: **Satan**

**(SCRIBE)** We know the Bible describes Abraham and Job as blameless. Read Genesis 6:9 and Luke 1:5-6. Who are described as blameless or just (depending on the version)?

Answer: **Noah, and Zacharias and Elizabeth**

## - LESSON 12 -

# HANNAH: TEACHING BY EXAMPLE

Scripture Text: Samuel 1–2

 ## BEFORE THE EVENT:

It's been about 350 years after the Israelites left Egypt and about 300 years since the beginning of the period of the Judges. Samuel is the last judge and is a prophet of God who anoints the first two kings of Israel, Saul and David.

✦ Ruth (Ruth 1–4): The events of this Moabite woman who becomes an ancestor of Jesus take place during the period of the Judges.

 ## LESSON:

Think of a person who has been a good example in your life. Your father? Your mother? Your Sunday school teacher? What are some examples in his or her life that have motivated you to be a better person? In the Bible, Hannah is a God-fearing woman who teaches us through example many lessons simply by the way she lives her life.

We read about Hannah in the early chapters of 1 Samuel. There is a man named Elkanah who lives with his two wives in the mountains of Ephraim. Elkanah is from the tribe of Levi, but because Levi does not have its own land in Canaan as the other tribes of Israel do, the Levites live within the other tribes' territories. It may seem unusual today that Elkanah, like other Israelites back then, has two wives, and back then, God allowed it even though it was never part of His original plan (Genesis 2:18-25; Matthew 19:2-6). He doesn't allow it today, however.

Anyway, Elkanah's two wives are Hannah and Peninnah. Hannah is childless but Peninnah does have children, a fact that Peninnah enjoys flaunting in front of Hannah who wants children very badly. Peninnah is mean to Hannah, and her taunts constantly upset Hannah.

### (READ 1 SAMUEL 1:6-7)

Elkanah doesn't understand why his wife is so sad and asks her whether he is better than having ten sons. When Elkanah makes an offering in Shiloh, Israel's religious center where the tabernacle is located (Joshua

## BIBLE WORD OF THE DAY:

MINISTER

Definition: To attend to the needs of others; to serve (1 Samuel 2:18).

*"Then the devil left Him, and behold angels came and **ministered** to Him"* (Matthew 4:11).

## BIBLE VERSES

1 Samuel 1:6-7
1 Samuel 1:10-11
1 Samuel 1:20
1 Samuel 1:26-27
1 Samuel 2:26

## BIG IDEA

**(SCHOLAR)** Hannah's faith is exemplified by both her passionate prayers for a son and by her actions when that prayer is answered.

*(continued on next page...)*

18:1), he gives portions to Peninnah and her sons and daughters but to Hannah, Elkanah gives a double portion because he loves her so much. Perhaps Peninnah is jealous of Hannah and gets back at her by saying ugly things to Hannah. While in Shiloh, with Eli the priest watching from the entrance of the tabernacle, Hannah makes a plea to the Lord.

## (READ 1 SAMUEL 1:10-11)

As Hannah prays, Eli notices that her lips are moving but she's not speaking aloud. Eli mistakenly jumps to the conclusion that Hannah is drunk because it appears that way to him. After talking to Hannah, Eli quickly sees this is a woman desperate for a child, a woman whose faith in God is strong, knowing that He is the only one who can answer her prayers for a son.

## (READ 1 SAMUEL 1:20)

When Samuel is about three years old, Hannah honors her vow to the Lord and brings him to live with Eli in the house of the Lord.

## (READ 1 SAMUEL 1:26-27)

So even as a child, Samuel ministers or serves the Lord under Eli's careful guidance. During their annual trips to Shiloh, Hannah and Elkanah visit their son, and Hannah brings him a little robe that she made for him to wear over his linen garment, or ephod, worn by priests. Eli blesses the couple saying the Lord will bring them descendants because of her son that was given to the Lord. And the Lord does just that, giving Hannah three more sons and two daughters. Meanwhile, back at the house of the Lord…

## (READ 1 SAMUEL 2:26)

Through Hannah, we learn about the power of prayer when we pray for the right things. We learn about her great faith. We learn about her desire to seek God first and that she's richly blessed with more children by doing so. In turn, Samuel becomes a blessing to the Israelites and grows up to be a faithful prophet of God who leads His oft-errant people on the right path. We will learn more about Samuel when the Israelites demand a king like other nations, and Samuel anoints Israel's first two kings, Saul and David.

(SCRIBE) Hannah's example teaches us how to be a faithful follower of God.

# BRING IT UP

(SCHOLAR) How is Hannah an example when others are being mean to us?

(SCRIBE) Why do you think Peninnah is so mean to Hannah?

---

 ## BIBLE BASICS:

1. Who is Samuel's father? **Elkanah**
2. Where is Elkanah from? **Mountains of Ephraim**
3. What tribe is Elkanah from? **Levi**
4. Who are Elkanah's wives? **Hannah and Peninnah**
5. Why is Hannah sad? **She doesn't have children**

**WRITTEN FOR OUR LEARNING**

6. What is Hannah's vow? **If the Lord gives her a son, she will dedicate him to His service for his entire life**
7. Who watches Hannah praying to God? **Eli**
8. Why does Eli think Hannah is drunk? **As she prays, her lips move but he doesn't hear her voice**
9. What does the name *Samuel* mean? **Asked of the Lord**
10. When does Hannah take Samuel to live with Eli and begin his service to the Lord? **After Samuel is weaned, about three years old**
11. What does Hannah make for Samuel when she visits him? **A little robe**
12. How many more children do Hannah and Elkanah have after Samuel is born? **Three sons and two daughters**

---

# BESIDE THE POINT:

**(SCHOLAR)** Samuel is a Nazarite. The other two lifelong Nazarites mentioned in the Bible are Samson, whom we studied a couple of weeks ago, and John the Baptist in the New Testament. Using the Scriptures below as references, discuss what it means to be a Nazarite. Both men and women are allowed to take the Nazarite vow and usually serve a set period of time as opposed to a lifetime. In addition, compare the lives of these three men.

- Laws who make the Nazirite vow.....................Numbers 6:2-6
- Purpose of the Nazarite vow............................Numbers 6:1-2
- Samuel, Samson's & John's mothers barren........... 1 Samuel 1:2; Judges 13:2; Luke 1:7
- All 3 men's births pre-announced or prayed for.......1 Samuel 1:17; Judges 13:3; Luke 1:13
- Tribes of the 3 men................................... 1 Chronicles 6:26, 34; Judges 13:2; Luke 1:5
- Similar Scriptures comparing the growth of Samuel, John, and Jesus...1 Samuel 2:26; Luke 1:80; Luke 2:52

**(SCRIBE)** Samuel begins serving God at a very young age. With your class, list and discuss specific things the students can do to minister to others in the congregation. To extend this activity, encourage the students to actually do something on this list, such as sending a card to a shut-in or helping out in the nursery. After they do so, ask them to share their experience ministering to the congregation.

---

# BRING IT HOME:

**(SCHOLAR & SCRIBE)** Discuss with your parents and family members about the concept of ministering. Use the example of your minister, bringing up the different things he does to serve the needs of the congregation in addition to preaching from the pulpit.

---

# BEYOND THE LESSON:

**(SCHOLAR)** Hannah dedicated her son to a lifelong service to the Lord. Read Numbers 8:23-26. What is the age range during which Levite men must perform their priestly duties in the tabernacle of meeting? In which verse do you find this week's **BIBLE WORD OF THE DAY**?

Answer: **25–50 years; verse 26**

**(SCRIBE)** Read 1 Samuel 2:12. What **BIBLE WORD OF THE DAY** is used to describe Eli's wicked sons in this verse?

Answer: **Corrupt**

**(SCRIBE)** Read 1 Samuel 2:26 and Luke 2:52. Whose growth is described in each verse?

Answer: **Samuel, Jesus**

## - LESSON 13 -
# SAUL: HANDSOME LEADER WITH AN UGLY HEART

Scripture Text: 1 Samuel 8–9, 13–15

 ## BEFORE THE EVENT:

As 1 Samuel 2:26 tells us, Samuel "grew in stature and in favor both with the Lord and men." Meanwhile, Eli grew old, and his sons are so evil the Lord desires to kill them. A man of God tells Eli that his priestly family will be destroyed.

- Samuel's First Prophecy (1 Samuel 3): Three times, Samuel thinks Eli calls him but it's actually the Lord who reveals to Samuel the tragic end of Eli's family.
- The Philistines Capture the Ark of God (1 Samuel 4:1-11): Israel again battles the Philistines, who steal the Ark of the Covenant.
- Eli's Death (1 Samuel 4:12-18): Upon hearing the Philistines are in possession of the Ark, Eli falls backward off his seat and breaks his neck.
- The Ark's Travels within Philistia and Return to Israel (1 Samuel 5–6): Bad things happen to those in possession or in close proximity to the Ark, motivating the Philistines to pass it back to the Israelites.

Note: These events surrounding the capture and return of the Ark are covered in Lesson 14

 ## LESSON:

For more than 300 years, God's people have been ruled by a series of judges. The judges often bail the people out of the clutches of pagan nations where they've suffered the consequences of their sins—mainly turning their back on God and turning to false gods. These idol-worshipping nations also have something the Israelites want: a king. Now the elders of Israel approach Samuel to ask for a king instead of a judge to rule over them. They tell the aging judge they want to be like other nations. Samuel does not think this is a good idea and goes to God in prayer.

### (READ 1 SAMUEL 8:7-8)

In other words, Samuel shouldn't take it personally. As a prophet, Samuel serves as a mediator between God and His people, so he warns them about the pitfalls of having a king. He even warns again, emphasizing

 ## BIBLE WORD OF THE DAY:

TRANSGRESS

Definition: To sin, do wrong, or break the law (1 Samuel 15:24).

*"And Moses said, 'Now why do you **transgress** the command of the Lord? For this will not succeed'"* (Numbers 14:41).

## BIBLE VERSES

1 Samuel 8:7-8
1 Samuel 9:1-2
1 Samuel 13:13-14
1 Samuel 15:7-9

 ## BIG IDEA

**(SCHOLAR & SCRIBE)** God does not judge a man by his appearance but by his heart.

*(continued on next page...)*

that a king will not solve all their problems and will inevitably create new ones. But the people insist, and Samuel anoints their first king—a man from the tribe of Benjamin named Saul.

## (READ 1 SAMUEL 9:1-2)

Saul seems to have a lot going for him: tall, good-looking, from a good family, in the prime of his life. By appearances, Saul looks like a leader, a king. By God's standards, Saul doesn't. That's because God looks at the "heart" of a person—his thoughts, capacity for sympathy, feelings and affection, emotions, etc. Saul is not a "man after God's heart." At first, Saul is humble and leads Israel in a few military victories. However the shallowness of Saul's faith in God becomes evident when he chooses to serve himself instead of God. The earliest example involves Saul's bad decision to assume the role of a priest, offering a burnt offering at Gilgal even though Samuel specifically told Saul to wait on him to do so. Not only does an impatient Saul disregard the instructions from the prophet of God, he also disobeys the law of God as only Levites are allowed to make sacrifices. When Samuel arrives to see what Saul has done, he asks how he could commit such a sin. Saul offers only excuses and not even a trace of repentance. So Samuel offers this prophecy regarding the end of Saul's reign as king:

(SCHOLAR & SCRIBE) Partial obedience of God's commandment equals full disobedience.

## BRING IT UP

(SCHOLAR) Why do you think God grants the people's desire for a king?

(SCRIBE) Why do you think Samuel prays to God after the people ask him for a king?

## (READ 1 SAMUEL 13:13-14)

That "man after His own heart" is David. This doesn't mean David is sinless but that he desires above all to serve God and follow His will. From this point, Saul has his eye on David and becomes increasingly envious of David as he becomes successful in battle and popular among the people. Envy turns to hate, and on several occasions—including a time David plays the harp to soothe Saul's nerves—Saul tries to kill him. It's an obsession that drives Saul into madness.

Meanwhile, Saul's sins continue to mount up. The last straw is when Saul blatantly disobeys a direct command of God: Attack Amalek, utterly destroy all they have, and do not spare them. Everyone and every animal are to be killed. Saul gathers an army of more than 200,000 men to destroy Amalek.

## (READ 1 SAMUEL 15:7-9)

Apparently, Saul doesn't follow directions very well. What Saul wants is more important than what God wants. Saul, not God, knows what's best for His people. He announces to Samuel that he has performed "the commandment of the Lord." Hearing the bleating of the sheep and lowing of the oxen taken from Amalek, Samuel asks why he disobeyed the voice of the Lord. Saul argues that he obeyed God even as he says he brought the king back alive, as well as the animals. He justifies saving the animals because they can be sacrificed to God. Finally, Samuel tells him: "Because you have rejected the word of the Lord, He also has rejected you from being king."

Those stinging words prompt Saul into sudden repentance. He begs Samuel for forgiveness. But it's too late. God has left Saul, and Samuel tells him he is leaving, never to return to Saul. As Samuel turns to leave, Saul pleads with Samuel, grabbing and tearing the edge of Samuel's robe. Samuel says, "The Lord has torn the kingdom of Israel from you today, and has given it to a neighbor of yours, who is better than you." That neighbor is David.

## BIBLE BASICS:

1. How long are the Israelites under the judges? **More than 300 years**
2. What is the sin the Israelites continue to repeat, leading them to suffer God's punishment? **Worship of idols**
3. For what do the elders of Israel ask Samuel? **A king**
4. Why do the Israelites want a king? **To be like the other nations**
5. Who goes to God in prayer about the matter? **Samuel**
6. God tells Samuel that their desire for a king is actually a rejection of whom? **God**
7. From what tribe is the first king of Israel? **Benjamin**
8. After what sin of Saul does God decide to end his kingship and choose a man after God's heart? **Saul's taking on the role of a priest, which is reserved for the Levites, when he offers a burnt offering at Gilgal**
9. Who does Saul try to kill several times? **David**
10. What nation does God command Saul to utterly destroy? **Amalek**
11. In what two ways does Saul not follow God's command regarding Amalek? **He spares the life of King Agag and the lives of their best animals**
12. Who becomes the second king of Israel? **David**

## BESIDE THE POINT:

**(SCHOLAR & SCRIBE)** Read aloud Deuteronomy 17:14-20 about God's commandments regarding kings. Explain that having a king to rule over Israel is not sinful in and of itself; however, God makes the rules for the kings as stated in this passage. Assign the following questions about the passage to each student so they can practice researching God's Word to find the answers. Students in the **SCRIBE** level may need the verse that contains the answer while **SCHOLARS** should be able to peruse the entire passage to find each answer.

1. In verse 14, there were no kings in Israel at the time, but what does this verse say will happen in the future? **The people will ask for a king, like the other nations around them**
2. In verse 15, God says Israel's king must not be what? **Foreigner**
3. In verse 16, God says Israel's king must not multiply what for himself and not cause the people to return to Egypt to multiply? **Horses**
4. In verse 17, why does God command that Israel's kings not multiply wives? **So they won't turn away from the Lord**
5. In verse 18, what is the king of Israel commanded to write? **A copy of this law in a book**
6. In verse 19, why is the king of Israel commanded to read this book? **So that he may learn to fear**

**SAUL: HANDSOME LEADER WITH AN UGLY HEART**

God and be careful to observe all of the laws and statutes

7. In verse 20, what does "that his heart may not be lifted above his brethren" mean? **If he fears God and observes His laws, the king will remain grounded, not believing he is above God's law and not thinking he is better than anybody else**

8. In verse 20, if the king fears God, observes all of His laws and doesn't turn away from His commandments, what will happen? **God will lengthen the days of his kingdom**

9. *Discuss with the class*: After reading what God says about Israel's kings, does Saul follow His laws as king and in what ways does Saul break these rules? Does God lengthen or shorten the days of Saul's kingdom?

**(SCHOLAR & SCRIBE)** Amalek is not some random country that God wants Israel to "utterly destroy." There's a specific reason behind God's command. Read Exodus 17:8-16 aloud with the class and assign the following questions to the students, to help them practice their Bible research skills.

1. In verse 8, where does Amalek attack Israel? **Rephidim**
2. In verse 9, what does Moses tell Joshua to do? **Choose men to fight Amalek**
3. In verse 9, what does Moses tell Joshua he plans to do? **Stand on the top of the hill with the rod of God in his hand**
4. In verse 10, who goes to the top of the hill with Moses? **Aaron and Hur**
5. In verse 11, what happens when Moses holds up his hand? **Israel prevails over Amalek**
6. In verse 11, what happens when Moses lets down his hand? **Amalek prevails over Israel**
7. In verse 12, who supports Moses' hands when he becomes weary? **Aaron and Hur**
8. In verse 12, how long are Moses' hands held up? **Until sunset**
9. In verse 13, who leads the battle? **Joshua**
10. In verse 14, what does the Lord want Moses to write in addition to a recount of the Amalekite attack on Israel? **God will utterly blot out the remembrance of Amalek from under heaven**
11. In Genesis 36:1, 12, who is an ancestor of the people of Amalek? **Esau**
12. In Deuteronomy 25:19, what warning to Amalek is repeated? **The Lord will blot out the remembrance of Amalek under heaven**
13. In 1 Samuel 15:2, what is the reason the Lord will utterly blot out the remembrance of Amalek? **For what he did to Israel: Ambushing Israel when the people first came out of Egypt**

# BRING IT HOME:

**(SCHOLAR & SCRIBE)** While the concept of people bowing to a statue and worshipping the false gods we read about in the Old Testament seems strange to us today, idolatry continues to be problem. Explain that idolatry is simply anything that takes precedence over God in our lives. Anything that's more important than worshipping and serving God is idolatry. Discuss with your parents and other family members what you learned about idolatry and some things that can become a form of idolatry if we're not careful.

 **BEYOND THE LESSON:**

**(SCHOLAR & SCRIBE)** After Samuel leaves Saul, the Lord tells Samuel to go to Jesse's house where He has chosen one of his sons to be the next king of Israel. When Samuel sees Jesse's oldest son Eliab he assumes that this must be the one. He's not. Read 1 Samuel 16:7. What two things does God say man looks at and the one thing He looks at?

Answer: **Appearance and physical stature; the heart**

**(SCHOLAR)** When Saul breaks the Lord's commandment by offering the burnt offering at Gilgal, God decides that his kingdom will not continue and chooses David to succeed him as king. Read 2 Samuel 7:16 and Psalm 89:3-4. How long will David's reign be?

Answer: **Forever**

**(SCRIBE)** This is not the first time Israel tries to have a king rule over them. Read Judges 8:22-23. Which judge, along with his son and grandson, do the people ask to rule over them?

Answer: **Gideon**

WRITTEN FOR OUR LEARNING

## - LESSON 14 -

# UZZAH: GOOD INTENTIONS WITHOUT OBEDIENCE DOES NOT PLEASE GOD

Scripture Text: 1 Samuel 4–6; 2 Samuel 6

 **BEFORE THE EVENT:**

The first king of Israel, Saul, dies and David prepares to succeed him. The Ark of the Covenant has been neglected, and David wants to bring it to Jerusalem, the new capital of the nation of Israel.

- Samuel Dies (1 Samuel 25:1): The prophet dies and is buried at his home in Ramah.
- Saul and the Medium (1 Samuel 28:3-25): Saul continues his spiral into sin and away from God when he asks for a séance in En Dor to drum up the spirit of Samuel.
- Saul and Jonathan Die (1 Samuel 31:1-6): Jonathan, David's close friend, is killed by the Philistines while his father, Saul, ends his own life.

 **LESSON:**

One of the first things David sets out to do as the new king of Israel is bring the Ark of the Covenant back home. The Ark serves as a reminder to the people that the Lord is with them, and it's been a while since this holy symbol of God's presence was in the tabernacle where it belonged. That's because the Israelites sinned against God. We will get to that in a minute.

God had instructed Moses how to build the Ark of the Covenant, considered holy because it holds the original stone tablets bearing the Ten Commandments (Deuteronomy 10:5). Decorated in gold, the Ark is almost four feet long and a little over two feet wide and tall. There are laws regarding who oversees the Ark (Numbers 3:30, 31) and how to move or transport it (Exodus 25:14, 15). Descendants from the Levite family of Kohath are in charge of the Ark and are the only ones allowed to carry it using special poles. No one touches it or looks inside it.

Fast-forward about 350 years, but before David becomes king. Samuel is a young boy, Eli is an old man, and Israel is at war with the Philistines. The Philistines defeat Israel in battle, killing 4,000 men. Israel regroups and the leaders wonder why God didn't protect them from the Philistines. So they decide to take the Ark from the tabernacle in Shiloh

 **BIBLE WORD OF THE DAY:**

FEAR

Definition: Holy reverence or respect (Proverbs 1:7).

*"Now therefore, **fear** the Lord, serve Him in sincerity and in truth…"*
(Joshua 24:14).

**BIBLE VERSES**
1 Samuel 4:18
1 Samuel 4:21-22
1 Samuel 5:6-7
2 Samuel 6:3
Ecclesiastes 12:13

 **BIG IDEA**

**(SCHOLAR & SCRIBE)** Good intentions are not enough if you are not following God's laws.

*(continued on next page...)*

and bring it with them to the battlefield, wrongly believing the Ark itself will give them victory over the Philistines. It is common for pagan armies to march into battle holding up images of false gods to protect them from the enemies. Apparently, Israel forgets that the Ark is just a symbol of God's presence and that God is always with His people. Eli's sons Hophni and Phineas are also in on this bad plan. It proves to be devastating because this time 30,000 soldiers from Israel, including Eli's sons, are killed on the battlefield. Even worse, the Ark is captured by the Philistines (1 Samuel 4:10, 11). A messenger reports to a frail, elderly Eli whose "heart trembled for the Ark." The man tells Eli about the great loss of lives in the battle, the deaths of his sons, and the Philistines' capture of the Ark.

(SCHOLAR & SCRIBE) In order to please God, we must first fear Him, which leads us to full obedience.

## BRING IT UP

(SCHOLAR) Why do you think God is not happy with us when we don't follow His laws exactly according to His specifications?

(SCRIBE) Why do you think we should do what God says in the Bible?

### (READ 1 SAMUEL 4:18)

Meanwhile, Eli's daughter-in-law and Phineas' wife goes into labor and has a baby. It is a difficult delivery and she names her son Ichabod as she is dying.

### (READ 1 SAMUEL 4:21-22)

Oh, the places the Ark will go! First, the Ark lands in the Philistine city of Ashdod, at the house of Dagon, their chief god. They place the Ark of the Covenant next to the false idol. The next morning, they discover that Dagon had fallen on its face to the earth before the Ark. They put Dagon back in its place. The next morning, they find Dagon lying on the floor the same way again, except the head and palms of its hands are broken from the body, leaving only the torso intact.

### (READ 1 SAMUEL 5:6-7)

So, the people in Ashdod, whom the Lord inflicts with tumors, send the Ark to another Philistine city—Gath. There, God inflicts the men with tumors and causes great destruction. The people of Gath try to send it to Ekron, but the people there know of the devastation in Ashdod and Gath and refuse to accept it. Philistine leaders connect the dots, decide the Ark is nothing but bad news for them, and send it back to Israel via a cart and two milk cows. The cows head straight for the Levite city of Beth Shemesh. Because the men of Beth Shemesh look into the Ark—a direct violation of God's law—God strikes down more than 50,000 men of the city. The next stop for the Ark is Kirjath Jearim to the house of Abinadab. Retrieving the Ark and restoring it to its holy place were not important to the first king of Israel, Saul, who had turned his heart from God (1 Chronicles 13:3). But it is to King David who loves the Lord and wants to do the right thing. Unfortunately, he doesn't do it the right way.

### (READ 2 SAMUEL 6:3)

David and 30,000 chosen men of Israel form a parade, dancing and playing music along the way to the Ark's new home in Jerusalem. When they approach Nachon's threshing floor, the oxen pulling the cart stumble. Uzzah puts out his hand, taking hold of the Ark to keep it from falling off the cart. God's anger is aroused and He instantly kills Uzzah because of his error. David's anger is then aroused because he's angry with God for striking down Uzzah, whose body now lies next to the Ark. Then, David's anger goes away and the necessary fear of God takes over his heart. In awe of the Lord, David humbly realizes he must have a proper fear and reverence in order to obey Him. Fear and obedience must go together. The Ecclesiastes writer sums it up in this verse.

### (READ ECCLESIASTES 12:13)

---

 **BIBLE BASICS:**

1. To whom does God give laws concerning the Ark? **Moses**
2. The family in charge of the Ark is from which tribe of Israel? **Levi**
3. Who falls off his seat backward and breaks his neck upon hearing that the Philistines captured the Ark? **Eli**
4. Why does Eli's daughter-in-law name her son Ichabod? **The glory of God has departed from Israel because the Ark has been captured**
5. Who is allowed to touch the Ark and look inside it? **No one**
6. What is the first city where the Philistines take the Ark? **Ashdod**
7. What are broken off Dagon the second morning? **Its head and palms of its hands**
8. What does the Lord do to the people of Ashdod and the men of Gath? **Inflict them with tumors**
9. Which Philistine city refuses to accept the Ark? **Ekron**
10. What do the oxen do, causing Uzzah to steady the Ark? **Stumble**
11. Who becomes angry with God for killing Uzzah? **David**
12. What does David realize that he needs to obey God? **Fear**

---

 **BESIDE THE POINT:**

**(SCHOLAR & SCRIBE)** God supplies ample instructions concerning the Ark of the Covenant, and although he meant well, Uzzah is accountable to these laws, too. Ask the students look up and read the verses regarding the two laws broken by Uzzah and those accompanying the Ark. Look for the verses answering the specific questions: Who is instructed to carry or move the Ark? What is the procedure to move it? Older students may be able to use a concordance, finding the passages on their own. Others may need some guidance. Some Scriptures to consider are Deuteronomy 10:8, Numbers 3:30-31, 4:15, and 7:9, and Exodus 25:12-14.

**(SCHOLAR & SCRIBE)** To learn more specifics about the Ark, look up the following Scriptures.
- Other Names for the Ark of the Covenant...... 1 Samuel 3:3; Exodus 25:22
- The Ark's Importance and Purpose................Exodus 25:22; Joshua 3:11
- Inside the Ark.............................................Exodus 25:16; Deuteronomy 31:26; Exodus 16:33-34; Hebrews 9:4

### UZZAH: GOOD INTENTIONS WITHOUT OBEDIENCE

**(SCHOLAR & SCRIBE)** You may want to share with your students "the rest of the story" about the Ark's last leg of its journey to Jerusalem. Read 1 Chronicles 13:13-14 where the Ark remains in the house of Obed-Edom for the next three months. Then read 1 Chronicles 15:1-10 about David's preparations for its arrival in Jerusalem. 1 Chronicles 16:1-6 tell of the Ark being placed in the tabernacle that David had erected for it.

---

 # BRING IT HOME:

**(SCHOLAR & SCRIBE)** Discuss with your parents and family members the importance of doing what God wants us to do concerning both worship and service to Him. Emphasize that we should always worship the way God wants us to. Also, talk about how good intentions are not enough to please God.

---

 # BEYOND THE LESSON:

**(SCHOLAR)** David is a great warrior king, and at the time the Ark is brought to Jerusalem, the new capital of Israel, he finally defeats the Philistines (1 Chronicles 14). The Philistines have been a thorn in Israel's side since the days of Samson. Read 1 Samuel 17:48-51. Who is the dead Philistine?

Answer: **Goliath**

**(SCRIBE)** Read Exodus 25:10. What kind of wood does God command the Ark of the Covenant be made of?

Answer: **Acacia wood**

Then read Genesis 6:13-22, where God gives Noah specific instructions for another kind of ark. What type of wood does God command Noah to use?

Answer: **Gopher wood**

## - LESSON 15 -

# SOLOMON: WISDOM FOR THE AGES

Scripture Text: 1 Kings 3–11

## BEFORE THE EVENT:

After serving 40 years as Israel's king, David is near death, and his fourth son Adonijah exalts himself, declaring that he is now the king. David is unaware of this, but the prophet Nathan gives Bathsheba a heads up on Adonijah's antics, because he knew she would not want her own son Solomon displaced as his father's successor. David takes an oath declaring Solomon king, and Adonijah is later executed by the new king after David dies. David reigns with Solomon for about two years before David's death.

## LESSON:

Solomon can be compared to a runner in a spiritual marathon who has a good start but a bad finish. Obviously, long-distance runners must physically train their bodies for marathons. But they also have to mentally prepare their minds to keep their focus and "finish strong." In Solomon's case, he's the son and heir of David who certainly receives the best training to succeed his father on the throne and be a spiritual leader for God's people. However, somewhere along the way, Solomon loses his spiritual focus and takes his eyes off the course God intends for him to follow. Unfortunately, his later-in-life sins steer him off track and play a major role in the future of the Israelites, which we'll cover next week.

Solomon does get off to a good start though. Shortly after becoming king, God appears to him in a dream and asks him what he wants. Solomon replies with humility, saying he is young and inexperienced faced with the enormous task as the leader of His people. Which explains his answer to God:

### (READ 1 KINGS 3:9)

God is so pleased with Solomon's request for wisdom that God gives him "a wise and understanding heart," making him the wisest man ever to live. And, because Solomon does not ask God for riches and honor, God gives Solomon riches and honor, making him a king like no other in his time. God then reminds Solomon of one thing.

## BIBLE WORD OF THE DAY:

DISCERN

Definition: Discover by intellect; to distinguish or have knowledge of (1 Kings 3:11).

"...*A wise man's heart* **discerns** *both time and judgment*" (Ecclesiastes 8:5).

## BIBLE VERSES

1 Kings 3:9
1 Kings 3:13
1 Kings 3:23-25
1 Kings 10:9
1 Kings 8:60-61

## BIG IDEA

**(SCHOLAR)** Like Solomon's influence on the Queen of Sheba, we must use...

*(continued on next page...)*

**SOLOMON: WISDOM FOR THE AGES**

## (READ 1 KINGS 3:14)

Solomon uses his wisdom for God's glory. The news of his judgments spread throughout Israel, causing them to fear the king because the saw the wisdom of God in his administration of justice. One such judgment centers on the case of two women and a baby. The first woman tells Solomon that the second woman had stolen her baby. The two women live in the same house, and both gave birth to sons three days apart. The first woman says the other woman's son died during the night because the other woman laid on him. The first woman says the second then took the living son from her side in the middle of the night while she was asleep and put the second woman's dead son by her side instead. The next morning, the mother of the living son saw that her son had been replaced by the other woman's dead son. The other woman then insists that the woman's story is not so, and claims that she is the mother of the living baby. A classic case of "she said, she said."

...everything we have—our talents, abilities, possessions, etc.—to the glory of God.

**(SCRIBE)** Like Solomon's prayer for wisdom, when we seek God's kingdom first, He will bless us in so many ways.

## BRING IT UP

**(SCHOLAR)** Why do you think some people who have great riches and possessions fall away from God?

**(SCRIBE)** Why do you think God gives Solomon great riches in addition to wisdom?

## (READ 1 KINGS 3:23-25)

Immediately the real mother of the living son begs Solomon to give the baby to the other woman and not to kill him. Then the mother of the dead baby tells Solomon to go ahead and divide the baby. Solomon in his wisdom knows the real mother would be willing to give up her son to the other woman in order to save her son's life. By the women's starkly different reactions to Solomon's decision to divide the baby, he knows who is the real mother and gives the child to her.

Soon, men of all nations and the kings of the earth come to hear Solomon. His unsurpassed wisdom expands beyond his seat of justice as he composes 3,000 proverbs and 1,005 songs on a wide range of subjects, especially about nature. The Queen of Sheba hears about Solomon's wisdom and great riches and decides to see it for herself. She tests Solomon with questions, but none are too difficult for him to explain to the queen, who also sees Solomon's great wealth in the house he built, the food on his table, his servants, and his entryway up to the house of the Lord. She concludes that the reports she's heard about Solomon are indeed true, and then some. "The wisdom and prosperity exceed the fame of which I heard," she tells Solomon.

## (READ 1 KINGS 10:9)

Solomon's wisdom is one of two of his major legacies during his reign as king of Israel. The second is his construction of the temple, a magnificent and permanent house of the Lord that replaces the tabernacle that had served as God's dwelling place among the Israelites for more than 300 years when they came out of Egypt. As king, David began preparing for its construction and received the blueprint from God. Just as God told Moses exactly how the tabernacle would be built, He told David the same for the temple, which would be 8 times the size of the tabernacle. David knew he could not build the temple because he was a king of war, but God told David that his son Solomon would be the one to actually build it. After seven years of work, Solomon dedicates the new temple and offers this blessing for the people.

### (READ 1 KINGS 8:60-61)

Solomon's words, "The Lord is God; there is no other" will no longer be an outward declaration of what's in his heart later in his life. Next week, we will find out how the wisest man in the world makes very unwise decisions with bad consequences that will affect the entire nation of Israel.

---

 ## BIBLE BASICS:

1. Who becomes the third king of Israel? **Solomon**
2. What does God ask Solomon in a dream? **"What do you want?"**
3. What does Solomon say he wants? **"An understanding heart to judge Your people so I may discern between good and evil"; wisdom**
4. Besides wisdom, what does God give Solomon even though he didn't ask for them? **Riches and honor**
5. What is the disagreement between the two women who come to Solomon for judgment? **Who is the true mother of the living baby**
6. What does Solomon command in order to determine the real mother of the baby? **Divide the living child in half**
7. What does the real mother tell Solomon? **Let the other woman have the baby to save his life**
8. What royal leader visits Solomon to see if the reports of his wisdom and riches are true? **Queen of Sheba**
9. How long had the tabernacle served as God's dwelling place among His people? **More than 300 years**
10. What replaces the tabernacle? **The temple**
11. Who receives the plans to build the temple from God? **David**
12. Who actually builds the temple? **Solomon**

---

 ## BESIDE THE POINT:

**(SCHOLAR & SCRIBE)** Just like in the book of Job, common phrases in our vernacular today have their origins in the books of Proverbs and Ecclesiastes, both written by Solomon more than 2,500 years ago. No other book has been written by man that continues to be as relevant and powerful as the Bible. Look up the following verses written by Solomon to find the common phrase and discuss the meaning of each.

+ Ecclesiastes 8:15......**Eat, drink and be merry**
+ Proverbs 15:1..........**A soft answer turns away wrath**
+ Ecclesiastes 1:9........**There's nothing new under the sun**
+ Proverbs 16:18.........**Pride goes before a fall**
+ Ecclesiastes 3:1........**To everything there is a season**
+ Proverbs 26:17.........**To take a dog by the ears**

### SOLOMON: WISDOM FOR THE AGES

**(SCHOLAR & SCRIBE)** Solomon is the wisest and richest man who ever lived, immensely blessed by God as long as he walks in walks in His ways and keeps His statutes. By man's standards, Solomon should be happy, at least satisfied with his life. But in Ecclesiastes Solomon searches for the meaning of life, analyzing the purpose of his vast wealth, great achievements, endless pleasures, and unsurpassed wisdom. Solomon finds no true satisfaction or happiness in any of these. Read the following verses with your students that describe his quest for fulfillment and his conclusion for each.

1. Wealth/Possessions—Ecclesiastes 2:7-17; Conclusion—No profit under the sun (2:11), Hatred of life (2:17)
2. Achievements—Ecclesiastes 2:4-6; Conclusion—Vanity (2:11)
3. Pleasure—Ecclesiastes 2:1-3; Conclusion—Vanity (2:1)
4. Wisdom—Ecclesiastes 1:12-18; Conclusion—Much grief, increased sorrow (1:18)
5. Solomon's Conclusion of the Whole Matter: Ecclesiastes 12:13—Fear God and keep His commandments, for this is man's all

**(SCHOLAR)** Your students probably know that the Bible was written by about 40 different men through the inspiration of God. Explain that there are books that name the author, and others that don't. The authors of most of the books in the latter category have been determined in part by cross-referencing them with others by known authors from the same time period. Let your Bible scholars cross-reference verses in Ecclesiastes that give us hints of its author with others from 1 Kings. See if they come to the same conclusion as most scholars, that Solomon penned Ecclesiastes. In addition, show them this is another way the Bible as a whole is a perfect, God-inspired book as evidenced by the harmony of its 66 books. First hint: the author is the son of David, king in Jerusalem, Ecclesiastes 1:1

- Wisdom: Ecclesiastes 1:16 and 1 Kings 3:12
- No one does not sin: Ecclesiastes 7:20 and 1 Kings 8:46
- Wrote many proverbs: Ecclesiastes 12:9 and 1 Kings 4:32
- Understanding of plants and animals: Ecclesiastes 2:4-7 and 1 Kings 4:33
- Major building projects: Ecclesiastes 2:4-6 and 1 Kings 9:1-19
- Male and female servants: Ecclesiastes 2:7 and 1 Kings 9:20-23
- Silver and gold: Ecclesiastes 2:8 and 1 Kings 10:11-23

# BRING IT HOME:

**(SCHOLAR & SCRIBE)** Discuss with your parents and other family members about the difference between intelligence and wisdom—or how you can discern the two traits. Intelligence is acquiring and applying knowledge and skills. Wisdom is not only having knowledge, but also life experience and good judgment and being able to use those qualities to make sound decisions.

**(SCHOLAR & SCRIBE)** Discuss with your parents and family members the importance of doing what God wants us to do concerning worship and service to Him. Specifically talk about how good intentions are not enough to please God.

 **BEYOND THE LESSON:**

**(SCHOLAR)** Read Song of Solomon 3:6-7. Whose couch is perfumed with frankincense and myrrh? Where else in the Bible do we read about these fragrances?

Answer: **Solomon's; Matthew 2:11, frankincense and myrrh were two gifts from the wise men who visit baby Jesus and His mother Mary**

**(SCRIBE)** Solomon has 700 wives, which we'll discuss next week. With all those wives, Solomon knows a thing or two about women. Read Proverbs 27:15. To what does Solomon compare a nagging woman?

Answer: **A constant drip, drip, drip on a rainy day**

# - LESSON 16 -

# REHOBOAM AND JEROBOAM: GOD DIVIDES THE NATION

Scripture Text: 1 Kings 11–12, 14

 ## BEFORE THE EVENT:

The third king of the united nation of Israel is also the last. God blesses King Solomon with unsurpassed wisdom and riches. Although he seems to have it all, he loses his faith to God, causing the nation of Israel to lose it all.

 ## LESSON:

Last week, we talked about King Solomon, David's son who humbly asks God for wisdom to guide the children of Israel with an understanding heart and a discerning mind. Then, at the dedication of the great temple he built for God, Solomon tells the people, "Let your heart therefore be loyal to the Lord our God, to walk in His statues and keep His commandments." Unfortunately, years later, Solomon lets his heart become loyal to many false gods. The problem stems from the fact that Solomon has 700 wives or princesses and 300 concubines, a good many of them from foreign nations. This breaks two of God's stern commandments concerning marriage: 1. Do not take many wives (Deuteronomy 17:17) and 2. Do not intermarry with Canaanite women (Exodus 34:12-17). The reason: "Surely they will turn your hearts after their gods," the Lord says.

### (READ 1 KINGS 11:4-6)

A very unwise decision. And, it turns out, a very tragic one for the entire nation of Israel. The Lord becomes angry with Solomon for his sin of worshipping other gods and tells him that He will tear the kingdom away from him and give it to his servant. But He will not do it until after Solomon's death. For the sake of David, God will give one tribe to Solomon's son. That tribe is Judah, in the southern part of the nation of Israel. The tribe of Simeon had merged with Judah sometime earlier, and many Benjamites live there because its tribe is next door. But, in comparison to the other 10 tribes, Judah is small but important because it's home of the capital city of Jerusalem, where the temple is located.

Solomon dies, and his son Rehoboam becomes king. When the young king goes to Shechem to be crowned, Jeroboam—Solomon's one-time

 ## BIBLE WORD OF THE DAY:

YOKE

Definition: Oppression, subjection, servitude that is a burden (1 Kings 12:4).

*"It is good for a man to bear the yoke in his youth"* (Lamentations 3:27).

## BIBLE VERSES

1 Kings 11:4-6
1 Kings 12:11
1 Kings 12:15
1 Kings 12:22-24
1 Kings 14:22

 ## BIG IDEA

**(SCHOLAR)** One person's sin can have a devastating effect on others.

**(SCRIBE)** Leaders who put themselves before God will find themselves without God.

trusted official—leads a group to meet with the new king. Specifically, they fuss about the "heavy yoke" they bear because of Solomon. That is, the high taxes and burdensome servitude they've incurred to support Solomon's lifestyle and building projects. They want the new king to lighten their load and reduce their taxes. Before he decides on the matter, King Rehoboam consults two groups of advisors. The first group—older, experienced officials who were advisors for his father—tells Rehoboam to speak kindly to the people and be their servant and they will respond well in return to the king. Rehoboam then asks the other group—younger, newly appointed men who grew up with him—what they think about it.

## BRING IT UP

**(SCHOLAR)** How can one person's sin affect others?

**(SCRIBE)** Why do you think the Israelites keep repeating the sin of worshipping false gods?

## (READ 1 KINGS 12:11)

Can you guess which group's advice Rehoboam takes? Telling the people that he will make their burden even worse than his father did is the second tragic decision that leads to the division of Israel.

## (READ 1 KINGS 12:15)

Remember, this is part of God's plan, the covenant He made with Abraham several hundred years earlier. Anyway, the ten tribes in the north secede, or leave, Judah because they want no part of the house of David. Rehoboam wants to force the northern tribes by attacking them and starting a civil war in order to unify Israel. He gathers 180,000 men to fight against them.

## (READ 1 KINGS 12:22-24)

God's people are now divided into two nations: Judah and Israel. It doesn't take long for these newly separated nations, particularly their kings, to separate from God.

## (READ 1 KINGS 14:22)

Meanwhile in Israel, King Jeroboam worries about the people who head south to the temple in Jerusalem to worship. He frets when they are among their kinfolk in Judah that they will turn their allegiance back to the house of David and to King Rehoboam. He is determined not to lose his kingship. He must keep them from returning to Judah.

So, Jeroboam hatches a plan to keep the people in Israel by establishing two worship centers nearby in Bethel and Dan. The centerpiece for these places for the people of Israel to worship? A golden calf. Two of them, one in each city. He makes shrines in the high places and appoints priests from tribes other than Levi. Jeroboam invokes their history when he reveals the golden calves: "Here are your gods, O Israel, which brought you up from the land of Egypt!" Unfortunately, their history keeps repeating itself.

---

 **BIBLE BASICS:**

1. What does Solomon do that makes God angry? **Worship other gods**
2. Who turn Solomon's heart from God and to false gods? **Solomon's foreign wives**

82 **WRITTEN FOR OUR LEARNING**

3. As a result of Solomon's sin of idolatry, what does God do? **Tear the kingdom away from Solomon, dividing Israel**
4. What's the last straw for Jeroboam and the leaders of the ten tribes, causing them to split from Judah? **Rehoboam refuses to listen to them and makes their taxes higher and their servitude more difficult**
5. Who is Solomon's son who becomes king of Judah? **Rehoboam**
6. Who becomes the first king of the new nation of Israel? **Jeroboam**
7. What two tribes, or portions of tribes, live in Judah? **Simeon and Benjamin**
8. When the ten tribes secede to form their own nation, what does Rehoboam want to do? **Fight Israel, forcing them back into the kingdom**
9. How many men does Rehoboam gather to fight Israel? **180,000**
10. Who tells Rehoboam not to fight to get back the kingdom? **Shemaiah**
11. Why does Jeroboam set up two worship centers closer to them in Bethel and Dan? **He's afraid the people will go to worship in Jerusalem and turn against him and back to Judah and Rehoboam**
12. According to King Jeroboam, what are the people's gods? **The golden calves**

---

# BESIDE THE POINT:

**(SCHOLAR & SCRIBE)** If we are to learn anything from the children of Israel, it is that God does not let sin go unpunished. Such is the case of Jeroboam's sin, because of which God says He will "exterminate and destroy it from the face of the earth" (1 Kings 13:34). Read 1 Kings 14:1-17; 15:25-30) and discuss the following in class.

1. Why does Jeroboam's wife dress in disguise to see Ahijah? (vs. 1-4)
2. Who clues the nearly blind Ahijah in on the woman's identity? (vs. 5)
3. Who has "done more evil than all who were before you, for you have gone and made yourself other gods and molded images to provoke Me to anger?" (vs. 6-9)
4. What does Ahijah tell her regarding the house of Jeroboam? (vs. 10-13)
5. What happens to Nadab, the son of Jeroboam who succeeds him as king? (15:25-27)
6. When is God's promise to exterminate and destroy the house of Jeroboam complete? (vs. 28-30)

**(SCHOLAR & SCRIBE)** While Rehoboam got off to a better start spiritually than Jeroboam, he eventually treads the well-worn path to worship false gods. Read 2 Chronicles 12:1-14 and discuss the following in class.

1. Why does Shishak rise up and attack Judah? (vs. 1-5)
2. When Shemaiah tells Rehoboam and Judah's leaders that the Lord has left them in the hand of Shiskak, what is their reaction? (vs. 6)
3. Because they humble themselves, the Lord decides not to do what? (vs. 7)
4. Instead, what will the people become as a result of their sin? (vs. 8)
5. What does King Shiskak do to the temple? (vs. 9)

**REHOBOAM AND JEROBOAM: GOD DIVIDES THE NATION**

**6.** Why does the Bible say King Rehoboam did evil? (vs. 14)

# BRING IT HOME:

**(SCHOLAR & SCRIBE)** Discuss with your parents and other family members the concepts of division and unity by reading Luke 11:17. How does the idea of a "house divided" apply to the Israelites?

# BEYOND THE LESSON:

**(SCHOLAR)** Read 1 Kings 11:34-36. God through Ahijah the prophet tells Jeroboam His plan to give him rule over the 10 northern tribes. Why does God reserve Judah for Solomon's son?

Answer: **"That My servant David may always have a lamp before Me in Jerusalem, the city which I have chosen for Myself, to put My name there."**

Similarly, who is the Light in John 1:6-7?

Answer: **Christ**

**(SCRIBE)** The division of Israel into two nations may seem to come out of the blue. However, tensions and quarrels among the tribes have been brewing since the days of their ancestors the 12 sons of Jacob. Remember the brothers' jealousy and hateful actions toward Joseph in Genesis 37? Read Judges 20:12-14. What tribe decides to go to battle against the other tribes?

Answer: **Benjamin**

# - LESSON 17 -

# ELIJAH: WITH GOD ON HIS SIDE, IT'S NO CONTEST

Scripture Text: 1 Kings 16:29-34; 18–19

 ## BEFORE THE EVENT:

There are 19 kings in Israel, 20 in Judah who reign during the time of the divided kingdom. All of the kings of Israel are bad, that is, evil in the sight of the Lord. Most of the kings of Judah fall into that dismal category, as well, but a few do what is right in the eyes of the Lord. The kings of Judah continue the line of their ancestor David, the line of which will bring the Messiah several hundred years from this point. By contrast, in Israel kings are murdered by conspirators in search of power or their own evil acts bring on their downfall. This is evident in the early kings of Israel:

- Nadab (1 Kings 15:25-32): Jeroboam's son's sinfulness causes Israel to sin and he is killed by Baasha who also kills the entire house of Jeroboam, fulfilling the word of the Lord.
- Baasha (1 Kings 15:33-34; 1 Kings 16:1-7): The Lord makes Baasha's house like Jeroboam's: the dogs shall eat those who die in the city, and the birds shall eat whoever dies in the fields.
- Elah (1 Kings 16:8-14): Baasha's son is murdered while seated on his throne by his chariot commander Zimri.
- Zimri (1 Kings 16:15-20): Reigning only seven days, Zimri meets a fiery end after burning the king's house down on himself because of his sins.
- Omri (1 Kings 16:16-28): The father of the notorious King Ahab, he not only does evil in the eyes of the Lord, but he also does worse that all who were before him.

 ## LESSON:

Throughout the Old Testament, we read about different ways God's prophets try to stomp out their sin of idolatry and pagan worship. Perhaps the most unusual yet direct strategy to get the people to see the absurdity of false gods is the contest Elijah holds on Mount Carmel. It's at a time when Israel plummets to a new spiritual low, thanks to a series of immoral and idol-worshipping kings, each more evil than the one before him. One of the most colorful and interesting characters in the Bible, Elijah serves as God's prophet when Ahab is king of Israel, who is more evil than his father Omri. He marries a foreign princess

 ## BIBLE WORD OF THE DAY:

ALTAR

Definition: Structure or platform on which to offerings and sacrifices (1 Kings 18:30).

*"Then the Lord appeared to Abram and said, 'To your descendants I will give this land.' And there he built an **altar** to the Lord, who had appeared to him"* (Genesis 12:7).

## BIBLE VERSES

1 Kings 16:32-33
1 Kings 18:20-21
1 Kings 18:27-28
1 Kings 18:36-37
1 Kings 19:14

 ## BIG IDEA

**(SCHOLAR & SCRIBE)** God is greater than any number of people who are against us.

Jezebel, who is also a priestess of the Canaanite god Baal. Ahab is easily influenced by his domineering wife and becomes a big fan of Baal.

## (READ 1 KINGS 16:32-33)

Elijah certainly has his work cut out for him. He meets with King Ahab, telling him that him and his father's house have forsaken the commandments of the Lord and have followed Baal. Then Elijah invites him, as well as 450 prophets of Baal and 400 prophets of Asherah (the fertility goddess) who eat at Jezebel's table, to join him on Mount Carmel. Jezebel is not only a major supporter of these false prophets but she is also a major enemy of God's prophets, having already slaughtered many of them and causing others to flee and hide from her in caves.

## (READ 1 KINGS 18:20-21)

Elijah then explains the rules of the contest. There are two teams: Elijah as a lone prophet of the Lord, and 450 prophets of Baal. Each side will choose a bull, cut it into pieces, and lay it on the wood. No fire is allowed under it. Each side then calls on its god or on the Lord, and the god who answers by fire is the real God. Elijah lets the Baal team go first. After they prepare the bull and place it on the altar, they start chanting, "O Baal, hear us!" And they keep chanting and calling for Baal from morning until noon, but no one answers. They even start leaping on the altar, apparently to get the Baal's attention.

## BRING IT UP

**(SCHOLAR)** Besides executing the 450 false prophets, what are some other possible reasons that Jezebel has to want to kill Elijah?

**(SCRIBE)** What do you think is going through Elijah's mind while he's watching the false prophets make spectacles of themselves on Mount Carmel?

## (READ 1 KINGS 18:27-28)

After the false prophets are through making a spectacle of themselves with no response from Baal, Elijah goes to bat. He calls the people of Israel to him as he sets about repairing an altar once used by their ancestors who worshipped God. He takes 12 stones, each representing the tribes of Israel, to build the altar and then makes a large trench around it. He puts the wood in order and places the prepared bull on it. Water is poured all over the burnt sacrifice of the bull and the wood on the altar three times, until it overflows into the trench. He wants them to see that what is about to happen is not some sort of magic trick.

## (READ 1 KINGS 18:36-37)

Then, the fire from the Lord falls and not only burns up the sacrifice and wood but also the stones and the dust. Basically, the fire destroyed everything including the water in the trench surrounding the altar. No doubt about who the winner is as His supernal power is witnessed by the people of Israel who fall on their faces, saying, "The Lord is God!" Their hearts have turned back to God. The Bible doesn't say how the prophets of Baal react to all this, but you can imagine them slinking away from the crowd in order to avoid another challenge from Elijah. Talk about sore losers. As it turns out, their lack of sportsmanship is the last thing on Elijah's mind when he orders the people to seize the false prophets. Elijah takes the false prophets to Brook Kishon where he kills them all by the sword.

King Ahab reports to his wife the events on Mount Carmel. Jezebel is furious when she learns that Elijah killed the prophets of Baal. So the evil Jezebel issues a death warrant for Elijah. When Elijah finds out the queen wants to kill him, he flees for his life, just as other prophets of God had done earlier. After a day of running from Jezebel, Elijah rests under a broom tree. He prays that the Lord takes his life. He falls asleep and an angel touches him and tells him to wake up and eat. He sees a cake and water and eats and drinks and goes back to sleep. The angel visits a second time, saying he needs to eat and drink some more. Elijah eats enough to sustain his 40-day journey to Horeb, the mountain of God, where he rests in a cave. God asks why he is here.

### (READ 1 KINGS 19:14)

The Lord instructs the weary Elijah to go to the Wilderness of Damascus where he will anoint the new king of Syria and the new king of Israel. Also, Elijah will anoint Elisha, the prophet who will take his place.

---

 ## BIBLE BASICS:

1. Where does Elijah's contest with the Baal prophets take place? **Mount Carmel**
2. How many false prophets are invited to Mount Carmel? **450 prophets of Baal and 400 prophets of Asherah**
3. Who is particularly close to these false prophets? **Jezebel**
4. What is the contest? **The one who answers the call of the prophets by fire is the true God**
5. What does Elijah repair? **An old altar that had been used by the people of God**
6. How many stones does Elijah use to build the altar? **12**
7. What does the fire from the Lord do? **Burns up the sacrifice, the wood, and consumes everything around it, including the water**
8. What happens to the false prophets after the contest? **Elijah kills them**
9. How do the people of Israel react to the fire from God? **They fall on their faces and say, "The Lord is God!"**
10. Who is angry that Elijah killed Baal's prophets? **Jezebel**
11. To where does Elijah escape? **Horeb**
12. Who does Elijah anoint to take his place? **Elisha**

---

 ## BESIDE THE POINT:

**(SCHOLAR & SCRIBE)** Read and discuss the event of Elijah taken up to heaven by a whirlwind (2 Kings 2:1-17). Consider the following as you lead the discussion.

1. Why do you think the author reveals the fact God is about to take Elijah up into heaven in the first verse, before it happens?
2. What does Elisha promise Elijah three times?
3. Compare the similarities and differences of Elijah's parting the Jordan River and Moses' doing the same at the Red Sea.

### ELIJAH: WITH GOD ON HIS SIDE, IT'S NO CONTEST

4. How does Elijah answer Elisha's request for a double portion of his spirit?
5. Describe how Elijah is taken up into heaven.
6. What does Elisha take that had fallen from Elijah? Discuss how the phrase is common is today's language.
7. What do the men who had received the revelation from God that Elijah would be taken up into heaven do after he is taken up into heaven?

**(SCHOLAR & SCRIBE)** Read and discuss the events of the blinded Syrians in 2 Kings 6:8-23.
1. Who is the "spy" who tells the king of Israel about the Syrians' plans?
2. What does Elisha allow his servant to see to reassure him?
3. What does Elisha pray that God do to the Syrians who are upon them?
4. Where does Elisha lead the blinded Syrian soldiers?
5. After their sight is restored, who asks whether or not to kill them?
6. Instead of killing the soldiers, what does Elisha do for them?
7. After sending the Syrians back home, who no longer comes to Israel?

# BRING IT HOME:

**(SCHOLAR & SCRIBE)** Romans 8:31 says, "If God is for us, who can be against us?" Elijah's challenge for the false prophets on Mount Carmel is visual evidence of His power. While God does not demonstrate His power in such a direct manner anymore, He has given us the Bible that reveals His power to us. Read this verse together with your parents, discussing the different ways His power can work through us today.

# BEYOND THE LESSON:

**(SCHOLAR)** Read 2 Kings 2:20-23. Who is Elijah's successor and mocked for being bald?

Answer: **Elisha**

**(SCRIBE)** Elijah is one of two people in the Bible who does not die on earth. Read Genesis 5:21-24. Who is the other person? Who is his son (the oldest person ever to live)?

Answer: **Enoch; Methuselah who lives 969 years**

**WRITTEN FOR OUR LEARNING**

## LESSON 18

# NAAMAN: A CHILD SHALL LEAD HIM

Scripture Text: 2 Kings 5

 ## BEFORE THE EVENT:

- Elijah is taken up into heaven by a whirlwind, leaving Elisha to continue in the Lord's work serving as His prophet. He performs miracles, such as purifying a bowl of water. Some young people make fun of Elisha for this, even calling him "baldhead." Elisha pronounces a curse on them for their mockery of the Lord and two female bears come out of the woods and maul 42 of the youths.
- Jehoram (2 Kings 3): The son of Ahab puts away the sacred pillar of Baal but persists in other sins worthy of the "evil" category among Israel's kings.
- More Miracles (2 Kings 4): Elisha performs more miracles in the name of the Lord, including raising the Shunammite's son and purifying a pot of stew.

 ## LESSON:

We've been talking about the Divided Kingdom and how God's people continue to disobey Him in so many ways, particularly in their worship of false gods. God sends prophets to urge them to repent and turn back to Him, but overall, the people don't listen. The kings in the northern kingdom of Israel and all but a handful of kings in southern Judah are rotten spiritual examples for the people, too. For the most part, they are "evil" leaders who forget God's covenant with Abraham and do things that are not pleasing to God.

But there are some of God's people who remain faithful during this bleak period in Israel's history. Such is the case of a young Jewish girl who does something that is pleasing to God. You will be surprised to learn how her faith profoundly changes the life of a great military leader who comes from a wicked country where the people bow down to idols. That military leader's name is Naaman. He is a commander of the Syrian army who the Bible describes as "great and honorable." God has given victory to Syria because of Naaman who is "a mighty man of valor." This reminds us that God controls everything—in countries where He's worshipped and in countries where He's not. He reigns supreme everywhere!

 ## BIBLE WORD OF THE DAY:

### LEPER

Definition: A person afflicted with one of several serious skin diseases, such as leprosy (2 Kings 5:1).

*"Command the children of Israel that they put out of the camp every **leper**..."* (Numbers 5:2).

## BIBLE VERSES

2 Kings 5:2-4
2 Kings 5:9-10
2 Kings 5:14
2 Kings 5:27

 ## BIG IDEA

**(SCHOLAR)** Faith in God sometimes requires obedience that we don't understand.

**(SCRIBE)** You're never too young to tell others about God.

**NAAMAN: A CHILD SHALL LEAD HIM**

Anyway, Naaman has a lot going for him except for one thing. He is a leper, a person who suffers from a slowly progressive and incurable skin disease. Leprosy is an infectious disease that doesn't go away and is characterized by sores, scabs, and white spots. It's an awful disease. It's painful. It's embarrassing. And people stay away from lepers because they don't want to get leprosy themselves. (Today, thanks to modern medicine, leprosy is far less common.) Specific laws in Leviticus reveal how the children of Israel are to deal with someone with leprosy (Leviticus 13:45, 46). However, Naaman is not an Israelite. In fact, he's a Syrian army commander who doesn't believe in the true God. That is, until a young girl from Israel speaks up.

## BRING IT UP

**(SCHOLAR)** Why do you think Elisha does not meet with Naaman when he comes to be healed of his leprosy?

**(SCRIBE)** What are some things that might have influenced the Jewish girl to be a faithful believer of God at such a young age?

## (READ 2 KINGS 5:2-4)

Apparently, the Jewish girl hears about Naaman's disease and she tells Naaman's wife about Elisha the prophet of God who could heal him. Imagine the courage of that little girl, probably close to your age, who is taken captive—perhaps separated from her family in Israel—to live in a strange country and work as a servant. I wonder if she is scared to live in a foreign country with people who don't believe in God? If so, that doesn't stop her from boldly telling Naaman's wife about Elisha. Her confidence and faith in God obviously makes an impression because his wife tells Naaman about this prophet. Before you know it, Naaman gets permission from the Syrian king to go to Israel to check it out. Elisha looks forward to Naaman's arrival in Israel.

## (READ 2 KINGS 5:9-10)

Naaman's reaction? He's furious! Naaman has the idea that Elisha should come out to him, wave his hand over the leprous area, call on the name of the Lord his God, and heal him of his disease in an elaborate act worthy of a great leader such as Naaman. Not a humiliating command from the prophet's messenger to wash in the Jordan River seven times. And then Naaman wonders what makes the Jordan so special. Why can't he wash in other rivers and be clean? After he calms down, his servants speak logically to Naaman, explaining that if Elisha told him to "do something great" that he would've done it, so why not do what he says, "Wash and be clean?"

## (READ 2 KINGS 5:14)

Naaman is not only happy his leprosy has vanished, but he recognizes who is behind this miracle and says, "I know that there is no God in all the earth, except in Israel." The young Jewish girl's words spoken to his wife eventually lead Naaman to believe in the one true living God of Israel.

The rest of this event involving Naaman focuses on the sin of greediness. Naaman is so grateful that he offers a gift to Elisha, and of course, Elisha refuses his gift and tells him to go home in peace. Elisha's servant Gehazi sees this as a wasted opportunity. Gehazi thinks if Elisha is not going to take Naaman's gifts, then he certainly will. So Gehazi runs after Naaman's chariot. When Gehazi catches up with him, Naaman naturally asks if everything is alright. Gehazi makes up a lie about some men of God needing a talent of silver (a large amount, about 70 pounds) and two changes of clothes. Naaman wants to help these men, who really don't exist except in Gehazi's greedy mind. So Naaman gives Gehazi two talents of silver and the clothes. When Gehazi comes home, Elisha asks him where he went. Not a smart idea to lie to God's prophet, but Gehazi does so anyway because he doesn't want Elisha to know about his meeting with Naaman on the road. "I didn't go anywhere," Gehazi answers. Of course, Elisha knows the truth.

### (READ 2 KINGS 5:27)

Quite a fitting punishment for a man who lets his greed for money rule his love for God.

---

## BIBLE BASICS:

1. What country is Naaman from? **Syria**
2. Who had given victory to Syria because of Naaman? **God**
3. Who tells Naaman's wife about a prophet who can heal Naaman of his leprosy? **Her servant, a young girl from Israel**
4. What are two reasons Naaman becomes furious? **Elisha himself does not meet him and he's told to simply wash in the Jordan instead of an elaborate healing act**
5. Who tells Naaman to wash in the Jordan River? **Elisha's messenger**
6. How many times is Naaman commanded to wash in the Jordan River? **7**
7. Who declares, "There is no God in all the earth, except in Israel?" **Naaman**
8. What does Naaman offer Elisha? **A gift for healing him**
9. Who wants Naaman's gift? **Gehazi, Elisha's servant**
10. What does Gehazi tell Naaman after he catches up with him? **A lie about two men who need a talent of silver and two changes of clothes**
11. When Elisha asks Gehazi where he went, what does Gehazi tell him? **He didn't go anywhere**
12. What happens to Gehazi after he lies to Elisha? **He becomes leprous**

---

## BESIDE THE POINT:

**(SCHOLAR & SCRIBE)** Elisha's servant Gehazi is not the only person the strikes with leprosy because of sin. Read and discuss two particular cases: Miriam, Moses' and Aaron's sister, in Numbers 12:1-16 and King Uzziah in 2 Chronicles 26:19-21. Describe the events leading up to their sins. Who is present? What are the sins they commit? What attitude do these two have prior to becoming leprous?

**(SCHOLAR & SCRIBE)** Most likely, the Jewish girl has no clue that by simply mentioning Elisha to Naaman's wife that it would lead to Naaman believing in the one true God. She is an example how we can spread the Word of God through conversation with the people in our daily lives. Initiate a discussion with your students how they can follow the Jewish girl's example on a regular basis. Come up with ideas how they can simply mention God, the Bible, what they learned in Sunday school, a song they sang in worship, etc. to others in daily conversation with their friends.

### NAAMAN: A CHILD SHALL LEAD HIM

# BRING IT HOME:

**(SCHOLAR & SCRIBE)** Discuss with your parents and other family members what you learned about Naaman. Compare how his physical cleansing of leprosy is symbolically similar to the spiritual cleansing of baptism. While there is nothing special about the water in the Jordan or the water in the church baptistry, the power and grace of God allow both Naaman and a believer in Him to be cleansed.

---

# BEYOND THE LESSON:

**(SCHOLAR)** The few verses that focus on Gehazi remind us about the sin of being "greedy for money" (Titus 1:7). Read Numbers 32:23. What does this verse say about sin and how does it relate in Gehazi's case?

Answer: **"Your sin will find you out." Gehazi apparently thinks he could be dishonest to Naaman and get the silver and clothes for himself and he could be dishonest with Elisha about his whereabouts**

**(SCRIBE)** Read Luke 4:27. Jesus tells the crowd in the synagogue in Nazareth that in the time of Elisha, there were many who had leprosy. How many of those with leprosy then were healed? Who does Jesus say was healed?

Answer: **One; Naaman**

**(SCRIBE)** Besides healing Naaman of his leprosy, Elisha performs many miracles to proclaim the Lord to the people. Read 2 Kings 4:42-44. What does Elisha's miracle here remind you of?

Answer: **Jesus feeding the 5,000 (Matthew 14:13-21)**

## - LESSON 19 -

# ATHALIAH AND JOASH: THE INFANT KING GRANDMA FORGOT

Scripture Text: 2 Kings 11–12; 2 Chronicles 22:10-12, 23-24

 **BEFORE THE EVENT:**

In Judah, descendants of King David reign over the southern portion of the Divided Kingdom now known as Judah. Solomon's son Rehoboam reigns 17 years, and there is war between him and Jeroboam in Israel all of their days (2 Kings 14:30). Rehoboam ends his reign on a bad note "because he did not prepare his heart to seek the Lord" (2 Chronicles 12:14). His son Abijam (Abijah) does not fare any better, following in Rehoboam's sins. However, his son (and Rehoboam's grandson) Asa is a breath of fresh air and a hope for God's people as his heart is "loyal to the Lord all of his days" (2 Kings 15:14). He removes the idols his father made. War and conflict continue between Israel and Judah under Asa, but his son Jehoshaphat makes peace with Israel (2 Kings 22:44) and does what is "right in the eyes of the Lord."

Meanwhile in Israel, Ahab and Jezebel's wicked reign of terror comes to a gruesome end when Ahab is killed in battle and Jezebel is thrown out of a window (1 Kings 22:29-38; 2 Kings 9:30-37). Untold numbers of Ahab's household are killed by Jehu, who becomes king of Israel. Yet, at least one of Ahab's descendants survives—his daughter Athaliah.

 **LESSON:**

When I say the word *grandmother*, what immediately pops into your mind? Maybe you think about your own grandmother—or grandmothers—or an older woman whom you fondly think of as a grandmother. We like to think about a grandmother as being gentle, loving, generous, wise, thoughtful, and kind. Has a batch of homemade chocolate chip cookies fresh out of the oven waiting for you. Spoils you by letting you eat one before dinner. Answers to a fun nickname, like Nana, GiGi, or Meemaw. Enjoys hearing about the fascinating Old Testament lessons you've studied in Bible class. Truly, this kind of grandmother, and especially a God-fearing grandmother, is a special blessing. For Joash, his grandmother is the furthest thing from a blessing. She's a greedy, power-hungry murderer who for six years stole the throne of David from his rightful heirs.

 **BIBLE WORD OF THE DAY:**

WRATH

Definition: Intense anger, rage, or fury (2 Chronicles 24:18).

"*The princes of Judah are like those who remove a landmark; I will pour out My **wrath** on them like water*" (Hosea 5:10).

**BIBLE VERSES**

2 Samuel 7:12-13
2 Chronicles 22:3-4
2 Chronicles 22:11-12
2 Kings 11:13-14

 **BIG IDEA**

**(SCHOLAR)** Like He did with Abraham and David, God always keeps His promises to us.

**(SCRIBE)** God's goodness always triumphs over man's wickedness.

**ATHALIAH AND JOASH: THE INFANT KING GRANDMA FORGOT**

## (READ 2 SAMUEL 7:12-13)

This means that no matter what, God promises that David's descendants, male heirs, will always rule over His kingdom. That is, in Judah. This is an extension of God's covenant with Abraham hundreds of years earlier in which Christ, the King of kings, will be born specifically through the line of David. Yet, for a short time, it seems those plans are derailed, but, as we've seen over and over, God always keeps His promises. Athaliah is the evil grandmother who seemingly pulls God's plan off track.

## BRING IT UP

**(SCHOLAR)** What do you think is going through Athaliah's mind when she sees Joash being anointed as king?

**(SCRIBE)** Why do you think one of the first things King Joash wants to do is repair the temple?

It all starts with her father Ahab, the evil king of Israel, and his wife Jezebel, who influences Ahab to take up false idols such as Baal and brazenly disobeys God's commandments. She kills many of God's prophets and even tries to kill Elijah. We don't know for sure if Jezebel is Athaliah's mother, but she is at least her stepmother, and an apparent evil influence on Athaliah while she's growing up. In other words, Athaliah is just like her idol-worshipping parents and does not follow the true God. She marries the son of King Jehoshaphat of Judah. He is a good king whose heart "delights in the ways of the Lord" by tearing down the wooden images and high places of idol worship in Judah. Jehoshaphat's son's name is Jehoram. Jehoram becomes king of Judah after Jehoshaphat's death and with Athaliah has a son named Ahaziah who briefly becomes king of Judah after Jehoram's death.

## (READ 2 CHRONICLES 22:3-4)

Ahaziah dies. What happens next is perhaps the most un-grandmotherly thing ever: Athaliah murders all possible royal heirs to the throne. In other words, she kills her grandchildren. She figures that if Ahaziah's sons and all of her other grandchildren are dead, she can claim the throne in Judah herself. However, she misses one.

## (READ 2 CHRONICLES 22:11-12)

When Joash is seven years old, the priest Jehoiada brings his nephew out of hiding and anoints him king of Judah, much to the joy of the people of Judah. They celebrate and honor the long-lost young king.

## (READ 2 KINGS 11:13-14)

Jehoiada then orders that Athaliah be killed for her wicked acts against God and the house of David, which is now restored to the throne. One of the first things King Joash decides to do is repair the house of the Lord, which had been neglected during the reigns of his father and grandfather. He instructs the Levites, the tribe assigned to the care and operation of the temple and other priestly duties, to collect money from all of Israel to fund the repair. Joash also broke the altars and images in Judah, erasing the visual reminders of the false gods his evil grandmother Athaliah had endorsed for the people to follow. Joash's goodness is the product of Jehoiada's influence as a child and later as king since Jehoiada continues to be a close advisor to Joash.

Then Jehoiada dies. And with his death, Joash's desire to serve God dies. He soon turns to serving false gods and encourages the people to do so as well. He forgets all that God had done for him, how and why he became king of Judah. He even kills a man of God named Zechariah who pleads with Joash to return to God. That man, by the way, is his cousin, a son of his uncle Jehoiada. While Joash begins his 40-year reign righting the wrongs of his grandmother Athaliah, he ends it by becoming just like her, one who worships idols and kills family members for his own gain.

## BIBLE BASICS:

1. Who is Athaliah's father? **King Ahab of Israel**
2. Who is Jehoram's father? **King Jehoshaphat of Judah**
3. Who is Ahaziah? **King Jehoram and Athaliah's son**
4. When King Ahaziah dies, what does his mother Athaliah do so that she can become queen? **She kills her grandchildren and other royal heirs**
5. Which royal heir escapes Athaliah's evil plot? **Joash**
6. How does Joash survive Athaliah's massacre of her grandchildren? **His Aunt Jehoshabeath and Uncle Jehoiada took the infant Joash and hid him from her for six years**
7. How old is Joash when Jehoiada anoints him as king of Judah? **Seven**
8. What happens to Athaliah after Joash becomes king? **She is killed**
9. What does King Joash want to repair? **The temple of the Lord**
10. People from which tribe are responsible for collecting money in order to repair the temple? **Levi**
11. When does King Joash turn away from God and toward false gods? **After Jehoiada dies**
12. What does King Joash do to Jehoiada's son who tells the king because he has forsaken the Lord, the Lord will forsake him? **Joash kills him**

## BESIDE THE POINT:

**(SCHOLAR & SCRIBE)** This activity focuses on the seemingly confusing family tree of Joash. Using the Scriptures below, students get a better understanding of who's who in the young king's ancestry line, and how he is related to kings in both Israel and Judah. As you read the verses in class, draw a simple genealogy chart that shows each ancestor's relationship to Joash. Emphasize how Joash is a direct descendant of King David, a fulfillment of God's promise that David's family would always reign in Judah.

+ 2 Chronicles 21:1………**Jehoram is the son of Jehoshaphat, king of Judah**
+ 2 Chronicles 21:6………**Athaliah is the daughter of Ahab, king of Israel**
+ 2 Chronicles 21:5-6……**Jehoram is married to Athaliah**
+ 2 Kings 8:25-26…………**King Jehoram and Athaliah's son is Ahaziah**
+ 2 Chronicles 22:1-2……**Ahaziah becomes king of Judah**
+ 2 Chronicles 22:1.1……**Joash is the son of Ahaziah**
+ 2 Kings 11:2……………**Jehoshabeath is the aunt of Joash**
+ 2 Chronicles 22:11……**Jehoiada is the uncle of Joash**

**ATHALIAH AND JOASH: THE INFANT KING GRANDMA FORGOT**

✦ 2 Kings 11:12..............Joash becomes king of Judah

**BONUS**.....King Joash kills Zechariah, the son of Jehoiada, when Zechariah tells the king that God will leave him because of the king's sins against Him. What is the relationship of Joash and Zechariah? Answer: **They are cousins**

 # BRING IT HOME:

**(SCHOLAR & SCRIBE)** It's curious that King Jehoshaphat (for the most part, a good king who "prepared his heart to seek God") allows his son Jehoram to marry Athaliah, the daughter of evil Ahab. Jehoshaphat has to know that Athaliah, whose father and Jezebel are major proponents of graven images and false gods such as Baal, will also follow their pagan-filled path that led them so far away from the true God. Discuss with your parents why it's important to know the religious background of the person you might marry one day. Pray with them that the parents and others who influence the young person you'll someday marry rear him or her in a faithful Christian household.

 # BEYOND THE LESSON:

**(SCHOLAR)** While Athaliah apparently does not revel in the role of doting grandmother, she's not the only grandmother the Bible singles out as being less than admirable. Read 2 Chronicles 13:2 and 15:16. Who loses her esteemed position as queen mother because she made an image of the false goddess Asherah?

Answer: **Maachah (Michaiah)**

**(SCHOLAR & SCRIBE)** In 2 Chronicles 23:13, Athaliah tears her clothes when she witnesses the people rejoicing over Joash becoming the new king of Judah. We've read about others who tear their clothes as an outward show of sorrow and pain. However, not many of them are women. Read 2 Samuel 13:19. Who is David's daughter that tears her robe of many colors?

Answer: **Tamar**

**(SCRIBE)** Joash is not the only king who begins his reign while still a boy. Another boy, whom the Bible says does "right in the sight of the Lord and walked in the ways of his father David," becomes king of Judah at age 8. Read 2 Chronicles 34:1. Who is this young king?

Answer: **Josiah**

# - LESSON 20 -
# JONAH AND NAHUM: THE REST OF THE STORY

Scripture Text: Jonah 1–4; Nahum 1–3

##  BEFORE THE EVENT:

A few years after the death of King Joash in Judah, King Jereboam II begins his rule over Israel around 782 B.C. Jonah, along with Amos and Hosea, serve Israel as God's prophets when Israel is on the cusp of succumbing to the mighty Assyrian nation, which comes to pass in 712 B.C. Like the other books of the Old Testament prophets, Amos and Hosea record their efforts to warn the people of Israel of God's impending judgment if they do not repent and return to Him. Jonah on the other hand is different. It's about a reluctant prophet whom God tells to go to a pagan nation, calling them to repentance. Specifically, Jonah's assignment is to warn the people of Ninevah, the capital of Assyria—a brutal, pagan nation that has been a thorn in Israel's side for many years.

##  LESSON:

God's covenant with Abraham continues to endure for hundreds of years as God never fails to keep His promises. However, the same cannot be said of the descendants of Abraham.

### (READ GENESIS 17:7-8)

Time and time again, generation after generation, Abraham's descendants do not want God to be their God. God responds by sending prophets to urge them to repent and warn them of God's punishment if they don't. When they do have a change of heart, it's usually not long before they return to worshipping false gods, disregarding God's laws and forgetting all that He has done for them. Now God calls on a prophet to preach to a foreign city where the people have never known about God.

### (READ JONAH 1:1-2)

You've probably heard of Jonah and remember how he was swallowed by a big fish. But you may not be familiar with Ninevah. It's the capital city of Assyria, the most powerful country in the world. Assyria is especially known for its cruelty against other nations. The Assyrians don't simply take over another country; they brutally kill some, savagely torture and force the rest into slavery. Jonah does not want to go to Ninevah to try to

## BIBLE WORD OF THE DAY:

VENGEANCE

Definition: Punishment or retribution for an injury or wrong (Nahum 1:2).

"…*Behold your God will come with **vengeance**, with the recompense of God; He will come and save you*" (Isaiah 35:4).

## BIBLE VERSES

Genesis 17:7-8
Jonah 1:1-2
Proverbs 15:3
Jonah 1:9
Jonah 1:15-16
Jonah 4:2-4
Nahum 2:13

## BIG IDEA

**(SCHOLAR)** God is slow to anger and shows mercy to those who repent of their sins and follow His laws.

**JONAH AND NAHUM: THE REST OF THE STORY**

save these evil people who are not Abraham's descendants and thus not God's chosen people. What Jonah doesn't understand is that God's love and mercy isn't reserved just for His people; God loves all people, even the wicked people of Ninevah. So Jonah tries to get out of the job God calls him to do by getting away from Him. It seems Jonah also doesn't understand that you can't escape the presence of God.

### (READ PROVERBS 15:3)

What follows is a series of events put in place by the Lord to serve His purpose concerning his runaway prophet. Jonah flees to Tarshish, finds a ship going to the distant city of Joppa, pays the fare, and boards the ship. Soon he falls asleep, safely tucked away in the lowest part of the boat. Meanwhile, God sends a great wind on the sea, tossing the ship to and fro and causing great fear among the experienced sailors. As they desperately toss cargo into the water to keep the ship afloat by lightening its load, the sailors cry out to their gods to save them. The captain finds Jonah sleeping through all this, wakes him up, and urges him to call on his God, too. Trying to figure out who on the ship is the root cause of the storm, the sailors cast lots and the lot falls on Jonah. The sailors ask the one they believe is putting their lives at risk who he is.

### (READ JONAH 1:9)

Jonah knows God caused the storm because of him. The sailors know it, too, because Jonah had told them he was running from God. The sailors feverishly try to row the boat to shore against fierce waves that were becoming even more tempestuous. But it's no use. They then cry out to the Lord to save them. Jonah tells them sailors to throw him into the sea, and the sea will become calm. So they do.

### (READ JONAH 1:15-16)

God prepares a great fish to rescue the prophet from drowning. Then Jonah spends three days and three nights in time out in the fish's belly. Not long after the fish vomits Jonah onto dry land, God tells Jonah a second time to go Ninevah, urging them to turn away from their wickedness and believe in the true God. Jonah announces they have 40 days to do so or Ninevah will be overthrown. The people of Ninevah pay attention to Jonah's warning. So, God spares the city from destruction because of their repentance and belief in Him. Jonah is not a happy prophet. Oddly enough, he's angry because the people are doing what he told them to do.

### (READ JONAH 4:2-4)

Jonah decides to sit outside the city, pouting and waiting to see what will happen next. The Lord prepares a plant to grow and Jonah appreciates its shade from the sun. God then sends a worm to kill it, taking away Jonah's source of protection from the heat. Jonah's level of comfort gets worse as God sends a strong east wind that beats on Jonah's head, and he grows faint. Jonah wishes he were dead. God explains to Jonah about the value of people whom were made in His image and therefore more important than

---

**(SCRIBE)** God wants everyone to be saved but we make the decision whether or not to follow Him.

## BRING IT UP

**(SCHOLAR)** Compare the fluctuation of Jonah's "heart" in these instances: When God calls him to go to Ninevah; when he identifies himself to the sailors; when he prays while housed in the belly of the fish; and when the people of Ninevah believe in God.

**(SCRIBE)** Why do you think God uses a great fish to save Jonah and then makes him stay inside the fish for three days?

plants and animals. God is free to show love and mercy on whomever He wants, including Ninevah.

Now, for the rest of the story…Ninevah's newfound belief and devotion to God is short-lived, although Jonah himself does not live long enough to see it. About 70 years after God spares Ninevah, Israel falls, succumbing to the mighty Assyrians. So in 722 B.C. Israel is gone. God's people who aren't killed become slaves. God uses the wicked nation of Assyria as the ultimate punishment for His people because they refuse to give up their practice of serving false gods and disobeying God's laws.

About 50 years after the destruction of Israel, the prophet Nahum brings the message of God's judgment against Ninevah. Remember it was Ninevah and the entire Assyrian Empire that destroyed the nation of God's people, even though God allowed them to do so. Nevertheless, the pain and suffering inflicted on God's people—Abraham's family—is not soon forgotten by the Lord. And Nahum's message in no sugarcoated terms warns Ninevah that because of what they did to Israel, God will do even more to Ninevah.

### (READ NAHUM 2:1)

Nahum's prophecy becomes a reality in 612 B.C., when the city of Ninevah falls. As Nahum predicts and describes in the book's three short chapters, the great city is wiped off the face of the earth because of the unmatched fury of God's wrath. Three years later, the rest of the Assyrian Empire meets the same tragic end. God uses the Babylonian Empire to conquer Assyria to avenge His people.

---

 ## BIBLE BASICS:

1. Who does God tell to go to Ninevah? **Jonah**
2. Why does Jonah get on a ship going to Tarshish? **To get away from the presence of God**
3. When the sailors are crying out to their gods and throwing out cargo to lighten the ship's load, what is Jonah doing? **Sleeping within the lowest part of the ship**
4. When the captain wakes Jonah up, what does he tell Jonah to do? **Pray to his God**
5. What do the sailors do to determine the cause of their trouble? **Cast lots**
6. After the lot falls on him, how does Jonah identify himself to the sailors? **As a Hebrew who fears the Lord, the God of Heaven**
7. Who comes up with the suggestion to throw Jonah overboard, making the sea calm? **Jonah**
8. After the sea becomes calm and the storm over, who believes in God? **The sailors**
9. Jonah tells the people of Ninevah that the city will be overthrown in how many days? **40**
10. What is Jonah's reaction when the people of Ninevah believe in God? **He's angry**
11. What does God use to teach Jonah that His love and mercy extends to all people? **A plant and a worm**
12. Who warns the people of Ninevah over 100 years after Jonah that God will totally destroy them? **Nahum**

### JONAH AND NAHUM: THE REST OF THE STORY

# BESIDE THE POINT:

**(SCHOLAR)** Pretend that you are the editor for *The Ninevah News* or the news director for WNNS-TV (Ninevah's news station). You want to run a piece on a Hebrew named Jonah who has come to town. You assign your reporters to cover different aspects on this feature. Divide your class into pairs: one student is the reporter and the other is Jonah. You determine what part of Jonah's experience you want each reporter to ask Jonah specific questions about. Help them come up with "answerable" questions. (For example, if the reporter is interviewing Jonah while he sits outside Ninevah, the first question the reporter asks could be, "Why are you sitting outside of the city?" Jonah could respond, "I'm waiting to see what is going to happen to Ninevah." Then, a logical follow-up question for the reporter to ask Jonah might be, "Why are you concerned what happens to Ninevah?" Jonah might answer, "Because I'm a prophet of God and warned the people of Ninevah that God would destroy them in 40 days." Naturally, the reporter might then observe, "You seem angry, Jonah. Why?" Jonah might respond, "Because I don't think they deserve to be saved from God's wrath. That's why." Have each pair focus on a different part of Jonah's story, including Jonah fleeing from God, Jonah's reaction and the sailors' actions on the ship amid the tempest, Jonah being tossed into the sea and being swallowed by the great fish, Jonah sitting outside of Ninevah, and Jonah's reaction to the plant and the worm.

If you want, provide the questions for the reporter who will ask them to "Jonah" and write down his answers for his "story."

When each reporter has his "scoop" on Jonah, have each one present his story to the class, providing total team coverage of Jonah's visit to Ninevah. If you are doing a written feature for *The Ninevah News*, help them write their stories and organize them on large construction paper. Help them come up with appropriate headlines for their stories. While the reporters are working on their stories, have the "Jonahs" draw their "photographs" of them doing whatever it is they were interviewed about.

Or, for the broadcast version, let each reporter give his/her story in front of the class based on the facts from his/her interview with Jonah. Maybe let the reporter add a "sound bite," asking Jonah a question. The last story in their coverage should focus on the fact that God will spare Ninevah because the people believed in God.

**(SCRIBE)** A major lesson that Jonah learns is that God is in control of His creation. His sovereign control means that He can change parts of it to serve His purpose. Have your students look up the following verses in Jonah. Ask them two questions for each verse: 1) What does God prepare/send? 2) What is God's purpose for each?

- Jonah 1:4............**Great Wind**
- Jonah 1:17..........**Great Fish**
- Jonah 2:10..........**Great Fish Vomits Jonah on Land**
- Jonah 4:6............**Plant**
- Jonah 4:7............**Worm**
- Jonah 4:8............**East Wind**

# BRING IT HOME:

**(SCHOLAR & SCRIBE)** Jonah and the great fish is one of the most well-known accounts in the Bible and one of the first accounts very young children learn about in Sunday school. Discuss with your family the lesson Jonah learned about God's desire to want everyone to be saved and His disapproval of Jonah's self-righteous attitude. Do some people in the church behave like Jonah, selfishly believing that God's grace and mercy is only for them?

---

# ➡ BEYOND THE LESSON:

**(SCHOLAR)** Some critics do not believe that Jonah was swallowed by a fish, instead insisting the event never happened and is just a fable. Read Matthew 12:38-41. Explain why these critics are wrong.

Answer: **Jesus compares Jonah's time inside the belly of the great fish to His time in the grave before His resurrection. Jesus cites the experience of Jonah as an actual event apparently known to the scribes and Pharisees to whom he's speaking.**

**(SCRIBE)** We've discussed the sin of idol worship among the Israelites already in several lessons. They turn away from the true God and worship false gods. In this lesson, we see the reverse: The sailors on the ship put away their false gods and believe on the true God (Jonah 1:15-16). In Ninevah, the people heed Jonah's warning and believe in God (Jonah 3:5). While it's rampant in the Old Testament, idol-worship is also evident in New Testament times. Read Acts 17:22-23. What is the name of the false god Paul mentions here?

Answer: **The Unknown God**

## - LESSON 21 -

# HEZEKIAH: FAITH STRONG ENOUGH TO TURN BACK TIME

Scripture Text: 2 Kings 18–20; 2 Chronicles 29–33

 ## BEFORE THE EVENT:

As briefly mentioned last week, the nation of Israel meets its demise because the people would not walk in the ways of the Lord nor obey His commandments (Isaiah 42:23-25). Chief among Israel's sins is worshipping false gods. Hoshea is the last of the 19 kings (all bad) when Assyria invades Israel, and the total siege takes three years. Hezekiah becomes king of Judah during this time and is all too aware of the threat from the Assyrians who are nipping at Judah's heels.

 ## LESSON:

Good King Hezekiah is just what Judah needs at this critical point in the people's lives. Their cousins in the northern kingdom have just been overtaken by the massive Assyrian Empire, and the nation of Israel is no more. During the three-year Assyrian invasion of Israel, the people suffer at the hands of this pagan nation, many of them scattered to all corners of the empire and taken away into captivity, becoming slaves. God through his prophets—most recently Amos and Hosea—had warned them to correct their wicked behavior in serving idols and to return to the ways of the Lord. This is their punishment for not obeying God.

So, is Judah next? Certainly the thought weighs heavily on King Hezekiah's mind when he witnesses Israel's destruction. With the Assyrians taking up residence next-door in the former Northern Kingdom, the threat looms over Judah. But first things first. Hezekiah must clean house. His father King Ahaz did evil in the sight of the Lord during his 16-year reign, serving false gods and building molten images for the Baals, to name a few. Now there's a big mess to clean up, both physically and spiritually, because of the sins of his father.

### (READ 2 CHRONICLES 29:4-6)

But it is much more than simply taking out the trash. There is a lot of work to be done, including removing the debris and everything related to the idols Ahaz had placed in God's house. And the holy articles and places within the temple need cleansing because they had fallen into

## BIBLE WORD OF THE DAY:

SANCTIFY

Definition: Set apart or declare as holy (2 Chronicles 29:5).

*"And I will **sanctify** My great name, which has been profaned in their midst…"*
(Ezekiel 36:23).

## BIBLE VERSES

2 Chronicles 29:4-6
2 Chronicles 31:20-21
2 Chronicles 32:7-8
2 Kings 19:35-37
2 Kings 20:9-11

## BIG IDEA

**(SCHOLAR)** Success comes to those who seek God first.
**(SCRIBE)** Like Hezekiah, we should develop a habit of prayer.

disrepair over the years. Throughout Jerusalem, Hezekiah tears down the high places for idol-worship and destroys the images the people served during Ahaz's reign. Hezekiah then focuses on the restoration of proper worship of the Lord. He reinstates the priests from the house of Levi so they can resume taking charge of operation of the temple and overseeing the burnt offerings according to the law God gave Moses.

## (READ 2 CHRONICLES 31:20-21)

Hezekiah then turns his attention to King Sennacherib of Assyria who has turned up the threat against Judah a few notches. He attacks and overthrows the fortified cities of Judah and now has his sights on Jerusalem. Perhaps Sennacherib thinks he can bully King Hezekiah by taunting him. He boasts of his empire's victories and mocks God, saying He's as powerless as the gods of the many nations Assyria has conquered. Hezekiah is a strong military leader, so he prepares the city for battle, repairing and building up the wall around Jerusalem, building another wall around that one, and raising the towers. He makes more weapons and shields.

## (READ 2 CHRONICLES 32:7-8)

Then King Sennacherib sends a threatening letter to King Hezekiah, heightening the possibility of Assyrian invasion of Jerusalem. Immediately, Hezekiah takes the letter to the Lord and prays for guidance and deliverance. God assures Hezekiah through the prophet Isaiah that Sennacherib will not come into the city, not even shoot an arrow within it. God will defend Jerusalem.

## (READ 2 KINGS 19:35-37)

During this time Hezekiah gets sick, so sick that he is near death. Isaiah tells him to set his house in order because he's about to die. Immediately, Hezekiah prays to God as he weeps bitterly. God tells Isaiah to go to Hezekiah, saying He heard his prayer and will heal him. God will add 15 years to Hezekiah's life and promises to defend Jerusalem from the king of Assyria. Hezekiah asks the prophet for a sign assuring these things will come to pass.

## (READ 2 KINGS 20:9-11)

No good king of Judah is without his flaws. And Hezekiah makes a mistake that will have a far-reaching impact on Judah. Hezekiah is on the mend from his near-death illness when the son of the Babylonian king pays him a visit, even bringing Hezekiah a get-well-soon present because he heard he had been sick. During the visit with the prince and his envoy, Hezekiah decides to give them a tour of his house to show off his impressive array of treasures. Silver and gold, spices and precious ointments are among the valued possessions of which he's proud. To show off your wealth to leaders of another nation, possibly a nation that could be an enemy, is not a wise thing to do. Isaiah discovers what Hezekiah did and scolds him, saying that these treasures will soon be carried off to Babylon, leaving nothing. And they will carry

## BRING IT UP

**(SCHOLAR)** Read 2 Kings 17:24-29. When the Assyrians settle in Samaria—the conquered Israel's capital—they do not fear the Lord. So, the Lord sends lions that kill some of them. After the king of Assyria figures out the lions were sent by the God of the land as punishment because the new pagan residents do not know Him, the king commands that a priest from Israel come there to live and instruct them about the worship of the God of Israel. Considering verse 29, what do you think happens as a results?

**(SCRIBE)** Why do you think Hezekiah is such a good king considering he had such an evil man, King Ahaz, as a father?

off some of Hezekiah's sons. After Isaiah finishes speaking, Hezekiah acknowledges his foolish error.

## BIBLE BASICS:

1. What nation conquers Israel? **Assyria**
2. What nation is under threat by the Assyrians? **Judah**
3. Who is the good king of Judah, son of the evil Ahaz? **Hezekiah**
4. What project does Hezekiah undertake as king? **Cleaning house spiritually and physically, ridding the nation of idols and restoring proper worship**
5. Who is the king of Assyria? **Sennacherib**
6. To whom does Sennacherib compare God? **The gods of the other nations Assyria has conquered**
7. What does Hezekiah take to the Lord when he prays for Jerusalem's protection against Assyria? **King Sennacherib's letter**
8. What does Assyria invade and take over? **The fortified cities in Judah**
9. When Hezekiah is sick and near death, what does he do? **He prays**
10. What two promises does God make to Hezekiah concerning his health and the safety of Jerusalem? **His life will be extended 15 years and the Lord will defend Jerusalem**
11. What is the sign that these things will happen? **The shadow going backward 10 degrees**
12. What is Hezekiah's foolish mistake? **Showing off his wealth and treasures to the Babylonian leaders**

## BESIDE THE POINT:

**(SCHOLAR & SCRIBE)** Because of Hezekiah's sin of showing off his treasures to the Babylonian prince, Isaiah tells him those same treasures will be taken by the Babylonians to their country. In addition, some of Hezekiah's sons will also be taken away to Babylonian. That very thing happens to Hezekiah's son Manasseh during his 55-year reign.

Manasseh is born during Hezekiah's 15 life-extending years and is only 12 years old when he becomes king of Judah. In spite of having such a God-fearing father, Manasseh does "much evil in the sight of the Lord to provoke Him to anger." Here's a short list of Manasseh's abominations against the Lord (2 Kings 21:3-9):

+ Rebuilt the high places Hezekiah had torn down
+ Raised up altars and made a wooden image for Baal as Ahab had done
+ Served Baal and other false gods
+ Built altars for the false gods in the house of the Lord
+ Practiced soothsaying, used witchcraft, and consulted mediums
+ Shed very much innocent blood

### HEZEKIAH: FAITH STRONG ENOUGH TO TURN BACK TIME

To sum it up, Manasseh acted more wickedly than all the Amorites who were before him. Manasseh is the most evil of all. Further, because Manasseh also had enticed Judah to sin with his idols, the Lord simply had enough and issues the ultimate judgment on Judah.

### (READ 2 KINGS 21:12-15)

Manasseh and the people refuse to hear the Lord who then sends Assyrian captains to seize Manasseh, binding him with hooks and fetters, and haul him off to Babylon, just as Isaiah had prophesied. While in prison, Manasseh has a change of heart—a major change of heart—and humbles himself before God and prays. God hears his prayer and restores the once-wicked king to the throne in Jerusalem. He is sincere about turning back to God. He removes the foreign gods and idols and the altars he built from the temple and out of the city, repairs the altar of the Lord, makes sacrifices and offerings, and commands the people of Judah "to serve the Lord God of Israel."

What are some lessons we can learn from Manasseh's repentance?

1. Although it's never too late for God to accept repentance, the consequences of the sins remain. (Even though he is sorry for his evil deeds, it does not erase that they ignited the Lord's anger to the degree that He will bring "such calamity upon Jerusalem and Judah").

2. It brings to mind Proverbs 22:6: "Train up a child in the way he should go, and when he is old he will not depart from it." (Good King Hezekiah apparently reared him to love God and keep His commandments until his death when Manasseh is 12. After living wickedly most of his life, Manasseh returns to his first love near the end.)

3. When studying the Bible, be sure to read all of the accounts of a person or event. (In 2 Kings 21:1-18, there is no mention of Manasseh's prison time in Babylon or subsequent repentance and restoration of Judah. But 2 Chronicles 33:1-17 includes "the rest of the story.")

## BRING IT HOME:

**(SCHOLAR & SCRIBE)** Discuss with your parents the sign the Lord gave Hezekiah concerning the extension of his life (2 Kings 20:8-11). With them, do some research to find out how much time as we measure time today (seconds, minutes, hours, days, etc.) equals the shadow that goes backwards 10 degrees. Learn about the sundials of Hezekiah's time and how they work.

## ➡ BEYOND THE LESSON:

**(SCHOLAR)** Read Numbers 21:6-9. The Israelites are complaining to Moses about having no food, no water, and other inconveniences in the wilderness. Because of their grumbling against the Lord and Moses, what does God send?

Answer: **Fiery serpents that bite the people**

After the people repent, the Lord tells Moses to make a fiery serpent and set it on a pole. Anyone who is bitten and looks at the serpent made of bronze would live. In 2 Kings 18:4, what does Hezekiah do to the bronze serpent and why?

Answer: **Hezekiah broke it into pieces because it had been turned into a false god by earlier generations of God's people**

**(SCRIBE)** Read 2 Kings 21:12 and Jeremiah 19:3 when God announces the future destruction of Judah because of the evil deeds of King Manasseh. Using context clues, what does "ears will tingle" mean?

Answer: **Ears will tingle because of the immense fear of those who hear such a harsh judgment**

## - LESSON 22 -

# JOSIAH: TAKING GOD'S WORD SERIOUSLY

Scripture Text: 2 Kings 22–24; 2 Chronicles 34–36

 ## BEFORE THE EVENT:

Not much time has elapsed. A repentant Manasseh dies and his son Amon reigns in Jerusalem for two years. His is an evil reign, cut short when his servants conspire and kill him in his own house. His young son Josiah takes the throne, becoming the last Godly king of Judah.

While the nation of Israel is gone with the invasion of the Assyrian Empire, God's mercy and longsuffering keep Judah from meeting the same fate. For now that is. He promised good King Hezekiah that Judah's punishment would not occur during his lifetime. The evil deeds of his son Manasseh provoked the Lord to so much anger that He announces the destruction of the nation of His people.

### (READ 2 KINGS 21:12)

Now it's just a matter of time. The fortified cities in Judah are in the hands of the Assyrians who continue to nip at Judah's heels in attempts to destroy Jerusalem, the capital of Judah and location of the Lord's temple. After the dark days of the 55-year reign of Manasseh and the two years of his son Amon, the next king is a breath of fresh air: Josiah. After Amon is murdered by his servants, his 8-year-old son Josiah becomes king, serving 31 years.

### (READ 2 KINGS 22:2)

At 16, Josiah does something reminiscent of his great-grandfather King Hezekiah. He commits to put God first in his life. A few years later he cleans house…again. His father and grandfather had made a spiritual mess of Judah and Jerusalem, just like Hezekiah's father Ahaz had done. It is no small task: Young Josiah gets rid of the high places, altars, and the many carved images they crafted for idol worship, breaking them into pieces and scattering the dust on the graves of those who sacrificed on them. Like Hezekiah, Josiah then focuses on repairing the temple, sending his close aides Shaphan, Maaseiah, and Joah to oversee

## BIBLE WORD OF THE DAY:

CALAMITY

Definition: Event causing great and often sudden damage or distress (2 Kings 22:20).

"…*If there is **calamity** in a city, will not the Lord have done it?*"

(Amos 3:6).

## BIBLE VERSES

2 Kings 21:12
2 Kings 22:2
2 Chronicles 34:14
2 Chronicles 34:23-25
2 Chronicles 34:33
Jeremiah 25:6-7

## BIG IDEA

**(SCHOLAR)** Total service to God includes a proper respect for His Word.

*(continued on next page…)*

the project. There were other men in charge of particular aspects of restoration. Hilkiah, the chief priest, is among them.

## (READ 2 CHRONICLES 34:14)

This is a huge discovery! Shaphan the scribe reports on the finding to King Josiah and reads a portion of the Book of the Law of Moses to him. Josiah becomes upset, even tearing his clothes, because he realizes the people have long not been following the commands of God as revealed in the Book of the Law of Moses. He immediately sends Hilkiah, Shaphan, and a few others to ask the prophetess Huldah to see what all this means.

## (READ 2 CHRONICLES 34:23-25)

The Lord will delay the destruction of Judah because of King Josiah's humble reaction to the book. Because he weeps, tears his clothes, and has a tender heart, the calamity that God will bring on Judah will not occur until after Josiah dies. Then Josiah reads the book, which is the first five books of the Old Testament, to all the men of Judah—great and small—the inhabitants of Jerusalem, the priests and Levites. He makes a promise to God: to follow and keep His commandments with all his heart and soul as they are written in the book.

## (READ 2 CHRONICLES 34:33)

**(SCRIBE)** Children who live for God can have a great impact on others.

## BRING IT UP

**(SCHOLAR)** Why do you think the people of Judah refuse to give up their idols and turn their lives around, especially after they witnessed the destruction of Israel?

**(SCRIBE)** What do you think is going through the people's minds as they are taken from their homes and forcibly taken as captives to the far away land of Babylon?

Near the end of King Josiah's reign, Babylon takes over Assyria, which had conquered Israel over 100 years earlier. Remember Nahum predicted this and now it's happened. God uses Babylon to avenge the suffering that Assyria inflicted on Israel. Next door to the south, Josiah dies. His son Jehoahaz becomes his successor, but only for three months before he is taken hostage by the king of Egypt, never to return to Jerusalem. The next—and final—three kings of Judah do evil in the sight of the Lord and end up taken captive to Babylon by its king, Nebuchadnezzar.

When God brings the Babylonians up against His people in Jerusalem, the devastation is widespread. It's not a quick invasion, taking about two years before Judah finally succumbs to the Babylonians. Many are killed, those who escape the sword become captives carried off to Babylon, and precious treasures are taken from the Lord's temple, and the temple is burned. Jerusalem is utterly destroyed. About 15 years before God's punishment on Judah, the prophet Jeremiah warns them.

## (READ JEREMIAH 25:6-7)

But Jeremiah also gives them hope for the future. First of all, God will avenge Judah by punishing Babylon for their pain, suffering, and devastation. Secondly, Judah's stay in Babylon will be brief—just 70 years—at which time His people will return to the land He gave them through His covenant with Abraham.

 # BIBLE BASICS:

1. What nation has captured the fortified cities of Judah? **Assyria**
2. How does Josiah become king? **His father King Amon is murdered**
3. How old is Josiah when he becomes king? **8 years old**
4. What three things does Josiah do that is reminiscent of his great-grandfather Hezekiah? **Josiah puts God first, cleans up the land by removing everything associated with idol worship, and repairs the temple**
5. What does Hilkiah find in the temple? **The Book of the Law of Moses**
6. What does Josiah do when he hears they haven't been following the laws in the book? **He tears his clothes**
7. Who is consulted about the meaning of the Book of the Law of Moses? **Huldah**
8. Who will not see the calamity that will fall on Judah? **King Josiah**
9. What happens near the end of Josiah's reign? **Babylon takes over Assyria**
10. Besides being evil kings, what do the last three kings of Judah have in common? **They are taken captive to Babylon**
11. How long does it take for Babylon to completely conquer Judah? **About two years**
12. Who prophesies about the destruction of Judah and the 70-year captivity of His people in Babylon? **Jeremiah**

---

 # BESIDE THE POINT:

**(SCHOLAR & SCRIBE)** This activity introduces your students to some of the minor prophets they may not be familiar with, especially during the period of the Divided Kingdom.

- **Joel**: Served in Judah around the time of King Joash. Known for using a plague of locusts as an analogy of the Lord's coming judgement against people and plea for their return to him (Joel 1:1-4).
- **Amos**: A sheep breeder and fruit tender from Judah who served Israel around 50 years before the fall of Israel. He preaches against the rich who are oppressing the poor in Israel (Amos 4:1-3).
- **Habakkuk**: Prophet in Judah around the time of the fall of Ninevah (612 B.C.). He is recognized for asking God questions about His judgment and impending punishment on Judah (Habakkuk 1:12-14).
- **Zephaniah**: Prophet in Judah who is a contemporary of Habakkuk. He can be described as a good-news, bad-news prophet because he predicts the bad news of Judah's punishment from God but also shares the good news of repentance, illustrated during the 31-year reign of good King Josiah (Zephaniah 1:4-6; 2:1-3).

Read 2 Chronicles 36:15-16. Discuss the purpose of the prophets when they try to persuade the people to abandon their false gods and follow the true God.

**JOSIAH: TAKING GOD'S WORD SERIOUSLY**

# BRING IT HOME:

**(SCHOLAR & SCRIBE)** Discuss with your family the importance of taking God's Word seriously. In order to have proper respect for the Bible, we need to know first what the Bible says. Talk about ways to make sure you can do that as a family.

---

# ➔ BEYOND THE LESSON:

**(SCHOLAR)** Zedekiah is the last king of Judah, serving 11 years. Read 2 Kings 25:4-7. What happens to him when the Babylonians invade Judah?

Answer: **His army flees from him and Zedekiah is captured and brought to Riblah where the Babylonians pronounce judgment on him. They kill Zedekiah's sons in front of him, put out his eyes, bind him with bronze fetters, and take him captive to Babylon**

**(SCRIBE)** Huldah is a prophetess, one of the few women mentioned in the Bible who serve in this special capacity for God. Read Exodus 15:20 and Judges 4:4. Who are two other prophetesses?

Answer: **Miriam, Deborah**

## - LESSON 23 -

# SHADRACH, MESHACH, AND ABEDNEGO: ON FIRE FOR THE LORD

Scripture Text: Daniel 1, 3

 **BEFORE THE EVENT:**

The last remaining stronghold in Judah, Jerusalem, falls in a two-year siege by the Babylonians, the most powerful nation in the world. In the years preceding Judah's destruction, Babylonian armies invade the country and carry many of God's people away as captives. This begins what Jeremiah had predicted as 70 years of Babylonian captivity.

 **LESSON:**

Josiah's son Jehoiakim is king of Judah during the first wave of the siege of Jerusalem by the Babylonian Empire. Nebuchadnezzar the king of Babylon takes King Jehoiakim as a prisoner. He also takes many of the young men of Judah to serve the king, but not just any young men. The king wants young men who meet a certain set of high standards: descendants of the king of Judah, good-looking in appearance, who are wise and knowledgeable with a quick understanding that will make them good candidates to learn the Babylonian language and literature. Among these men are Daniel and his three friends Shadrach, Meshach, and Abednego, all from the tribe of Judah. You've probably heard of them. The enduring faith of these God-fearing men is a reflection of how they live their daily lives.

For three years in the foreign country that had taken them as prisoners, Daniel and his friends undergo special training to thoroughly prepare them to serve the king. A big part of the daily regimen is their diet: the king's "delicacies"—special royal food forbidden under God's commandments and meat probably used in idol worship to the Babylonian gods. And they are given wine to drink.

### (READ DANIEL 1:8-9)

Like his ancestors Hezekiah and Josiah before him, Daniel puts God and His laws first in his life. But this poses a problem for the king's official who is in charge of the trainees' food program. If Daniel and his friends start to look pale and sickly, looking a lot older than the other young men, then the king might kill him for not doing his job. Daniel then poses a solution: Allow Daniel and Shadrach, Meshach, and Abednego

## BIBLE WORD OF THE DAY:

DEFILE

Definition: To make unclean or impure; pollute (Daniel 1:8).

*"But those things which proceed out of the mouth come from the heart, and they defile a man"* (Matthew 15:18).

## BIBLE VERSES

Daniel 1:8-9
Daniel 1:19-20
Daniel 3:4-6
Daniel 3:12
Daniel 3:17-18
Daniel 3:29

## BIG IDEA

**(SCHOLAR)** Our strong faith and unwavering confidence in God safely guides us through the fires in our lives.

to eat nothing but vegetables and water for ten days and compare their appearance with those who eat the king's food. The official agrees to the test, and sure enough, the four young men from Judah appear "better and fatter in flesh than all the young men who ate the portion of the king's delicacies." Point made; the official gives them only vegetables and water from then on. When their training is completed, Daniel and his friends appear before King Nebuchadnezzar.

### (READ DANIEL 1:19-20)

It's not long until they receive a promotion from the king, who is happy because Daniel interpreted his dream. Daniel becomes ruler over the province of Babylon and chief administrator over all the men of the country. At Daniel's request, Shadrach, Meshach, and Abednego are set over the affairs of the province of Babylon.

One day, King Nebuchadnezzar has an image of gold made of himself. This statue is close to 100 feet tall! When all of the officials of Babylon gather for the dedication of the huge golden statue of Nebuchadnezzar, a decree is set forth across the land.

### (READ DANIEL 3:4-6)

So no matter what, when they hear the horn, flute, harp, and lyre together, they must fall down and worship the golden image of King Nebuchadnezzar. Failure to do so means death in the fiery furnace. There are some Babylonian tattle-tales who don't like the Jews, particularly the king's officials Shadrach, Meshach, and Abednego, and use this decree against them.

### (READ DANIEL 3:12)

That's actually true: They don't serve the king's gods and do not worship the king's golden image. And never will, which is basically what they tell the furious king. The king wants to know which god will save them from the burning fiery furnace.

### (READ DANIEL 3:17-18)

Because their words stir up the king's anger to burn even more, he turns up the heat, making the furnace seven times hotter than usual. The men bind Shadrach, Meshach, and Abednego and cast them into the blazing furnace to their deaths. However, the ones who die are the men who experience the exceeding heat and overwhelming flames at the furnace door when they put them inside. God protects the three men of Judah amid the flames. The king is shocked as he watches them walk around in the furnace with a fourth who is "like the Son of God." He orders his men to bring them out, where his officials also witness that the fire had no power over them. They didn't even smell like smoke. Shadrach, Meshach, and Abednego's confidence and faith in God make quite an impression on Nebuchadnezzar who issues a new decree.

---

*(continued on next page...)*

**(SCRIBE)** Let others see our faith in God by the way we

## BRING IT UP

**(SCHOLAR)** How does Daniel show his spiritual strength when he is trained to serve the Babylonian king?

**(SCRIBE)** What tells you about a ruler who makes a big golden statue that looks like him for the people to worship?

### (READ DANIEL 3:29)

By the way, Shadrach, Meshach, and Abednego end up getting another promotion.

---

## BIBLE BASICS:

1. Besides King Jehoiakim, who else is taken captive during the first wave of the Babylonian invasions? **Daniel, Shadrach, Meshach, and Abednego**
2. Why are these four young men of Judah taken as captives? **To train them to serve the king**
3. What do Daniel and his friends refuse to eat? **The king's food**
4. Why do they refuse to eat the king's food? **Because it violates God's law**
5. How long is the training period? **Three years**
6. What test does Daniel propose concerning their food? **Allow Daniel and his friends to eat vegetables and water and compare their appearances with those who eat the king's food**
7. After 10 days, who looks better? **Daniel and his friends**
8. What does King Nebuchadnezzar make of himself? **A large gold image**
9. When the people hear the horn, flute, harp, and lyre together, what are they supposed to do according the decree? **Fall down and worship the golden image of Nebuchadnezzar**
10. Who doesn't fall down and worship the golden image of Nebuchadnezzar? **Shadrach, Meshach, and Abednego**
11. How many "people" does Nebuchadnezzar see in the furnace? **Four**
12. What new decree does Nebuchadnezzar issue after their God saves Shadrach, Meshach, and Abednego? **If anyone speaks against their God, he will cut him into pieces and his house will be made in an ash heap**

---

## BESIDE THE POINT:

**(SCHOLAR & SCRIBE)** What do you remember about Daniel and the lions' den in Daniel 6? Try to answer these questions without referring to the passage, but the verses are provided in case you want to check your answers.

1. Who is the king at the time Daniel is cast into the lions' den? **Darius** (vs. 1)
2. What position is Daniel in Darius' kingdom? **Governor** (vs. 2)
3. What does Daniel's enemies think is the only way to find fault with Daniel? **He would break the law of the land if it went against the law of God** (vs. 5)
4. What decree do Daniel's enemies talk Darius into making? **Anyone who prays to any or man but the king in the next 30 days will be thrown into the lions' den** (vs. 6-7)
5. What does Daniel do when he finds out about the king's decree? **He goes home and prays to God** (vs. 10)
6. Who do Daniel's enemies tell that Daniel disobeyed the decree? **Darius** (vs. 11-13)

**SHADRACH, MESHACH, AND ABEDNEGO: ON FIRE FOR THE LORD**

7. What is Darius' reaction when he finds out Daniel did not follow the decree? **He is upset and greatly distressed** (vs. 14)
8. What can no one do to a decree? **Change it** (vs. 15)
9. At night what can the king not do because of Daniel's situation? **Sleep** (vs. 19)
10. Who does Daniel say shut the lions' mouths? **An angel of God** (vs. 21)
11. What is the king's new commandment? **Daniel's accusers, as well at their wives and children, will be thrown into the lions' den** (vs. 24)
12. What is Darius' new decree concerning Daniel? **Men in every part of Darius' kingdom must tremble and fear before the God of Daniel**

## BRING IT HOME:

**(SCHOLAR & SCRIBE)** Many Daniel "stories" are well known and often learned during a child's preschool years. Write down the different lessons we can learn from each of these events in Daniel's life? Bring the list back to class and share with the class.

## BEYOND THE LESSON:

**(SCHOLAR)** Read Hosea 5:14, the prophet's warning to the people about Judah's punishment. What does Hosea compare God to?

Answer: **A young lion**

**(SCHOLAR)** Read Isaiah 43:1-2. Who is Isaiah referring to in the statement, "When you walk through the fire, you shall not be burned?"

Answer: **Israel**

**(SCRIBE)** Read 2 Samuel 23:20. What is unusual about the weather when David's army commander Benaiah kills a lion?

Answer: **It is a snowy day**

**(SCRIBE)** Read Genesis 3:2. What is on fire but not being burned?

Answer: **The burning bush**

# - LESSON 24 -

# EZRA AND NEHEMIAH: THE REMNANT RETURNS AND REBUILDS

Scripture Text: Ezra, Nehemiah

 ## BEFORE THE EVENT:

From the time the first wave of Israelites are carried off to Babylon until now, it's been 70 years. It's time for the remnant of Israel to return to Jerusalem.

 ## LESSON:

In *The Wizard of Oz*, Dorothy and her dog Toto have been far away from home for a long time. Dorothy makes some colorful friends and has some fun adventures with them. So much fun, in fact, they make a movie about it. Even so, Dorothy concludes that "there's no place like home" and can't wait to return. Certainly, that's how the children of Israel must feel when they find out they can return home to Judah where they have spent some 70 years in faraway Babylon not having such a fun time. They have been captives in a foreign country about 1,000 miles away—God's punishment for His wayward children who repeatedly chose to worship false gods and crafted images in place of Him. All along through His prophets, God had promised them they would return home, to the land He promised to Abraham and His descendants many years ago.

### (READ JEREMIAH 27:22)

About 100 years earlier, Isaiah prophesied that "the remnant will return, the remnant of Jacob, to the Mighty God." That remnant is those who are left over from the destruction of Israel and Judah and, with their children, return to Jerusalem after the Babylonian captivity. In all, about 50,000 people return. We read about their return in the books of Ezra and Nehemiah about 500 years before Christ is born.

Just as the surviving Israelites in Judah were carried away to Babylon in three stages (remember, Daniel was in the first wave of exiles to Babylon), the people return to Judah in three groups. This occurs over a period of about 100 years. The hand of the Lord is behind Cyrus the king of Persia who issues a decree allowing God's people to return to Jerusalem and rebuild the temple that was destroyed by the Babylonians. Persia, by the way, had recently conquered Babylon, avenging His people for Babylon's destruction of Judah and punishing the country for their wickedness

 ## BIBLE WORD OF THE DAY:

REMNANT

Definition: A small remaining quantity of something; remainder (Ezekiel 6:8).

*"The **remnant** will return, the **remnant** of Jacob, to the Mighty God"* (Isaiah 10:21).

## BIBLE VERSES

Jeremiah 27:22
Ezra 3:10-11
Ezra 4:12-13
Ezra 6:6-7
Ezra 9:10-12

 ## BIG IDEA

**(SCHOLAR)** The same God who kept His promise to the Israelites to return home to Judah will keep His promise to Christians by giving them a home in Heaven.

*(continued on next page...)*

(Jeremiah 25:12). King Cyrus also orders the return of the articles and treasures Nebuchadnezzar had stolen from the temple. So, the people receive a free pass to go back home and rebuild not only the temple but also the entire city that's now in ruins. A man named Zerubbabel, a direct descendant of King David, leads the first group of Israelites on the 1,000-mile journey from Persia (Babylon) to Judah. Within a couple of years, work on the temple begins.

## (READ EZRA 3:10-11)

**(SCRIBE)** God is stronger than anyone who opposes you when you work for Him.

## BRING IT UP

**(SCHOLAR & SCRIBE)** It was about a two months' journey (1,000 miles) from Persia to Judah. What do you think it was like for the children who made that long journey with their parents?

Not everybody shares their joy. The Samaritans in particular are not being nice neighbors as they try to discourage the Israelites and make it difficult for them to rebuild. They even write a letter to King Artaxerxes, complaining about "the inhabitants of Judah and Jerusalem."

## (READ EZRA 4:12-13)

The Samaritans' letter is effective, causing the king to order work on the temple to stop immediately. When work resumes under Zerubbabel and the prophets Haggai and Zechariah, the governor of the region questions their authority to do so. When the matter reaches the new king in town—Darius, he does some digging and discovers the initial decree King Cyrus had indeed set forth commanding the rebuilding of God's temple.

## (READ EZRA 6:6-7)

So, 21 years after work on the temple began, it's completed and the people celebrate the house of the Lord with joy (Ezra 6:16). About 80 years after the first group of Israelites arrive home, the second group departs Babylon-now-Persia led by the priest Ezra. Being a priest, of course, Ezra is a descendant of Aaron from the tribe of Levi. He's also a "skilled scribe in the Law of Moses…expert in the words of the commandments of the Lord and of His statutes to Israel." Just as God had done with Cyrus and Darius, He works through King Artaxerxes who allows Ezra extra money and supplies for the temple and gives him authority to set up a judicial system in Judah. The land of Judah is under the authority of the Persian government at this time, but the king allows Ezra to establish Judah's own system of justice and punishment. Ezra leads the people upon their return to follow the laws and commandments of God, encouraging them not to make the mistakes their ancestors did. Understandably, he becomes upset when he sees that already many have married those from pagan nations, nations who worship false gods. He goes to God in prayer, confessing the sins of the nation.

## (READ EZRA 9:10-12)

Many of those guilty of marrying those from pagan nations are moved by Ezra and give up their spouses in order to follow the Lord's commandment. This is part of Ezra's task to point the children of Israel back to God and His laws.

 **BIBLE BASICS:**

1. How many years have the people been in captivity in Babylon? **70**
2. What nation conquers Babylon? **Persia**
3. About how many Israelites return to Judah? **50,000**
4. In how many groups do the people return to Judah? **3**
5. Which king issues the decree to allow the people to return to Judah and rebuild the temple? **Cyrus**
6. Which king researches and finds the decree of Cyrus allowing them to return? **Darius**
7. Who leads the first group back to Judah? **Zerubbabel**
8. From which tribe is Zerubbabel, since he's a direct descendant of King David? **Judah**
9. What group of people causes the work on the temple to stall and eventually cease for many years? **Samaritans**
10. What two prophets work with Zerubbabel when work resumes on the temple? **Haggai and Zechariah**
11. Who leads the second group to Judah? **Ezra**
12. How is Ezra described? **Skilled scribe in the Law of Moses, expert in the words of the commandments of the Lord and of His statutes to Israel**

---

 **BESIDE THE POINT:**

**(SCHOLAR & SCRIBE)** Nehemiah is another key player in the work to rebuild and restore the Lord's people in Judah. Nehemiah is a cupbearer for the king who hears that while the temple has been rebuilt, the wall and gates of Jerusalem is a mess—broken down, burned and in ruins.

### (READ NEHEMIAH 1:4)

Nehemiah immediately prays to God. He requests permission to return to Jerusalem, rebuild the wall, and restore the city. Nehemiah's royal position in Artaxerxes' kingdom gives him a front row seat to the happenings in Persia and with the king personally. The king asks Nehemiah why he looks so sad.

### (READ NEHEMIAH 2:2-3)

King Artaxerxes then asks Nehemiah how he can help, and before you know it, Nehemiah has permission to go home to aid in the city's reconstruction, particularly its walls. The king also gives him supplies and letters for safe passage in the regions he'll go through on the way to Judah. After arriving with the third and final group of Israelites back to Judah, Nehemiah sees the crumbled rocks that once formed the great wall of Jerusalem.

### (READ NEHEMIAH 2:17-18)

**EZRA AND NEHEMIAH: THE REMNANT RETURNS AND REBUILDS**

Like Zerubbabel before him, Nehemiah feels the heat of opposition to the reconstruction of Jerusalem's walls. Nehemiah is mocked by those such as Sanballat, Tobiah, and Geshem.

### (READ NEHEMIAH 2:20)

Nehemiah speaks boldly to those who oppose God. They also use other tactics to slow down or stop the building of the walls, and each time, Nehemiah deflects their attacks with prayer and determination to do God's will. The wall, by the way, is completed in a remarkable 52 days! Nehemiah dedicates the wall (Nehemiah 12:27-43) and issues many reforms to encourage the people to continue to worship God and follow His commandments.

1. What is Nehemiah's position? **The king's cupbearer**
2. Why is Nehemiah sad? **The wall and gates of Jerusalem is in ruins**
3. How does Artaxerxes help Nehemiah? **Allows him to return to Judah, gives him supplies and letters to ensure a safe trip**
4. Who leads the third group of Israelites to Judah? **Nehemiah**
5. How long does it take to finish the wall? **52 days**

(SCHOLAR & SCRIBE) There's a lot of laughing in the Bible, such as Sanballat, Tobiah, and Geshem in Nehemiah 2:19: "…they laughed at us and despised us…." This does not mean something is funny, but it is a scornful or mocking laughter. Look up and read the following passages. Using context clues, decide the kind of laughter in each verse.

+ Psalm 37:12-13 (**Scornful**)
+ Genesis 18:10-15 (**Ridiculous**)
+ Ecclesiastes 3:4 (**Joy**)

---

 ## BRING IT HOME:

(SCHOLAR & SCRIBE) Read Ezra 7:10 with your parents and other family members. The Bible says Ezra had prepared his heart to seek the Law of the Lord. Compare Ezra's life to that of King Rehoboam as revealed in 2 Chronicles 12:14 who did not prepare his heart to seek the Lord. Discuss how you can prepare your heart to serve the Lord each day. Specifically, make a list on how to prepare your heart before you go to worship each Sunday.

---

 ## BEYOND THE LESSON:

(SCHOLAR) In Ezra 3:4, the people resume the observance of The Feast of the Tabernacles. Read Leviticus 23:41-43. What is the purpose of The Feast of the Tabernacles?

Answer: **Reminder of the time their ancestors spent living in the wilderness for 40 years after God brought them out of Egypt**

**(SCRIBE)** Nehemiah is King Artaxerxes' cupbearer, an officer of high rank in the kingdom. Read Nehemiah 2:1 and Genesis 40:11, 21. What is the main duty of the king's cupbearer? In Genesis, the cupbearer or butler here has a dream that is interpreted by whom?

Answer: **To fill the king's cup and present it to him personally; Joseph**

**WRITTEN FOR OUR LEARNING**

# - LESSON 25 -
# ESTHER: THE RIGHT PLACE AT THE RIGHT TIME

Scripture Text: Esther 2:19–9:28

 ## BEFORE THE EVENT:

The events of Esther take place during those in the books of Ezra and Nehemiah. While Ezra and Nehemiah focus on the return of the Jews after exile in Babylon-now-Persia, the book of Esther is about the Jews who stay in Persia, specifically during the reign of King Ahasuerus and his queen, Esther. This lesson begins after Queen Vashti is banished for refusing the king's command to appear before him and the nobles to show off her beauty. Esther becomes queen in a type of beauty contest to see who delights the king the most. Esther does not reveal to the king that she is a Jew.

 ## LESSON:

Esther is the only book in the Bible that does not contain the word *God*. However, we see that God is definitely present throughout the book, working behind the scenes to protect His people—now called Jews—and to accomplish His plan and purpose for them.

We'll begin the lesson near the end of chapter 2 when Esther becomes King Ahasuerus' queen. King Ahasuerus rules over the expansive and powerful Persian Empire. Esther is beautiful and Ahasuerus selected her from hundreds of women to be his queen. She's also a Jew, but the king doesn't know that. Her cousin Mordecai reared Esther and had told her not to reveal the fact she's a Jew.

### (READ ESTHER 2:21-22)

Bigthan and Teresh are hanged on the gallows as a result of Mordecai's actions to save the king's life, and the whole episode is recorded in the official book of the chronicles.

Besides King Ahasuerus, Queen Esther, and Mordecai, the other main character in the book of Esther is a royal official named Haman. Because Haman ranks above the princes, the king's servants within the king's gate bow and pay homage to him when he passes by them each day. Everyone, that is, except Mordecai. This made Haman, who's not a nice guy, really angry.

## BIBLE WORD OF THE DAY:

PERISH

Definition: To die; to suffer death in a sudden, violent way (Esther 4:16).

*"For the Lord knows the way of the righteous, but the way of the ungodly shall **perish**"* (Psalm 1:6).

## BIBLE VERSES
Esther 2:21-22
Esther 3:5-6
Esther 4:3
Esther 4:15-16
Esther 5:14
Esther 7:4-6

## BIG IDEA
**(SCHOLAR)** God works behind the scenes to put people in certain situations for His plan and purpose.

*(continued on next page...)*

### (READ ESTHER 3:5-6)

Haman wants to get rid of not just Mordecai, but all of the Jews because the Bible states Haman is an enemy of the Jews. So Haman devises an evil plot to do just that. He convinces Ahasuerus that the Jews within the Persian Empire do not keep the king's laws. To solve this problem, Haman suggests that the king issue a decree "to destroy, to kill, and to annihilate all the Jews, both young and old, little children and women, in one day." The king signs off on the decree and word goes out to all of the empires' 127 provinces that the Jews will be destroyed on the 13th day of the 12th month. Mordecai, along with the rest of the Jews in the Persian Empire, soon learn of the decree—and their fate—and are understandably upset.

### (READ ESTHER 4:3)

Esther herself is deeply distressed about the decree. Remember her husband the king does not know she is a Jew. Mordecai realizes that Esther is in an ideal position to help her people out of this terrible situation. Through a messenger, Mordecai urges Esther to intervene and talk to the king about stopping the impending massacre of the Jews. Esther at first is fearful because no one, not even the queen, approaches the king without an invitation. Esther would be risking her life if she goes to the king to discuss the matter. When Mordecai explains that her becoming queen in the first place may have been to protect the Jews from harm, Esther decides to risk her life and approach the king on behalf of her people.

(SCRIBE) When things seem hopeless, remember that God is always in control.

## BRING IT UP

(SCHOLAR) The children of Israel are first referred to as Hebrews, then Israelites, and now at the time of the Exile and thereafter, Jews. Why do you think they are called Jews?

(SCRIBE) How do you think Haman feels when King Ahasuerus tells him to honor Mordecai in the city square?

### (READ ESTHER 4:15-16)

Esther dresses up in her royal robes and boldly approaches the king with a request. While Ahasuerus tells her that he'll grant her "up to half the kingdom," she just asks him attend a banquet that she's prepared for him—and to bring Haman along, too. That must have struck Ahasuerus as an odd request. Anyway, at the banquet, the king asks Esther again what she wants, and again, she tells him that she'd like the king and Haman to come to another banquet the next day. Haman is so thrilled to be asked not once but twice to be her personal guest at her banquet. It makes him feel so important, which feeds his already puffed-up view of himself. But when he sees Mordecai at the king's gate and Mordecai does not bow to him, he becomes furious. That's all he can think about. His wife Zeresh and his friends come up with an idea to cheer up the selfish and self-centered Haman.

### (READ ESTHER 5:14)

That night, King Ahasuerus can't sleep. So he wants someone to read the book of the chronicles to him to help him nod off. The part read to him is the incident where Mordecai saved his life by reporting the plot of Bigthan and Teresh to kill him. The king wants to know if Mordecai has been honored for this, and since he hasn't, the king orders Haman, who thinks at first the king wants to honor him, to honor his mortal enemy Mordecai. Haman realizes that because the king is honoring Mordecai, who is a Jew, that can't be good for Haman. And he's right. At the banquet, Esther fills Ahasuerus in on what Haman has done—his plot to kill her people, the Jews.

**WRITTEN FOR OUR LEARNING**

### (READ ESTHER 7:4-6)

And Haman should be terrified, especially when the king's servants take hold of him and hang him on the gallows he planned for Mordecai. However, because a decree cannot be reversed, Esther and Mordecai write another decree in the king's name to allow the Jews to defend themselves on the day planned for their destruction.

### (READ ESTHER 9:5)

The Jews kill 75,000 of their enemies including the ten sons of Haman that day. They then establish as special feast called Purim to serve as a remembrance of this event.

---

## BIBLE BASICS:

1. What does King Ahasuerus rule over? **Persian Empire**
2. Who is Esther's cousin who raised her like a daughter? **Mordecai**
3. Why does Haman get angry at Mordecai? **He will not bow down to him**
4. When Haman discovers Mordecai is a Jew, what does he do? **Talks the king into issuing a decree to kill all of the Jews in the Persian Empire**
5. When are the Jews going to be destroyed according to the decree? **On the 13th day of the 12th month**
6. Who does Mordecai think can help the Jews from impending death? **Esther**
7. How many banquets does Esther invite Ahasuerus and Haman to? **Two**
8. Who talks Haman into building a gallows to hang Mordecai on? **His wife Zeresh and his friends**
9. Who is hanged on the gallows instead? **Haman**
10. Who writes the new decree to allow the Jews to protect themselves from those who seek to do them harm? **Esther and Mordecai**
11. How many enemies of the Jews are killed? **75,000**
12. What is the feast established to observe the events in the book of Esther? **Purim**

---

## BESIDE THE POINT:

**(SCHOLAR)** We do not know who wrote the book of Esther. Many historians believe that Mordecai is the author. What are some clues that could point to Mordecai as the author? Give the verse(s) to support each clue.

**(SCHOLAR)** In Esther 4:1, we read about Mordecai's reaction and physical display of grief after learning about the decree to destroy the Jews. Besides tearing his clothes, which we discussed in earlier lessons, Mordecai also put on sackcloth and ashes. Using your concordance or other reference aids in your Bible,

### ESTHER: THE RIGHT PLACE AT THE RIGHT TIME

find other examples of people putting on sackcloth and ashes. One example is found in Daniel 9:3.

**(SCRIBE)** Esther is a woman in the Bible with many admirable traits. Write the word *Esther* on the board vertically. As a class, come up with an adjective starting with each letter that describes Esther. Discuss the reason for each adjective based on what we know in the Bible.

**(SCRIBE)** Discuss the purpose of the Feast of Purim (Esther 9:18-28). Bring up secular holidays, such as Independence Day and Thanksgiving, and why we observe them to illustrate why the Jews are to observe Purim. You may also want to discuss the Lord's Supper, when and why it's observed.

##  BRING IT HOME:

**(SCHOLAR & SCRIBE)** In class, we end the lesson with Purim, how it became a feast to commemorate the God's deliverance of the Jews from destruction. There's one more thing we did not cover as a class—Mordecai. With your family, read Esther 10 and discover happens to Mordecai. Write down your answer and share it with your teacher and/or class next week.

##  BEYOND THE LESSON:

**(SCHOLAR)** The Bible does not say specifically why Mordecai refuses to bow down and pay homage to Haman. It could be because Haman is from a family that's a long-standing enemy of the Jews or because the gesture is a form of worship of a person of high rank in the kingdom. Read 1 Samuel 24:8. In what situation does God's law permit a person to bow down to a king?

Answer: **As David bows to King Saul, the gesture is used to show respect and honor to Saul's position as king**

**(SCRIBE)** Esther does not eat or drink—to fast—for three days before she approaches the king. Read Matthew 4:1-2. How long does Jesus fast while in the wilderness?

Answer: **40 days**

## - LESSON 26 -

# MALACHI: THE LAST WORD BEFORE THE WORD

Scripture Text: Malachi 1–4

 ## BEFORE THE EVENT:

In Ezra and Nehemiah, the remnant of the Jews return to Jerusalem to rebuild their home and reestablish their relationship with God. The second temple and the walls around the city are built. The prophets Haggai and Zechariah encourage renewal in their spiritual lives as they preach to the people about the Law of Moses and not reverting to sin, especially idolatry. Malachi comes on the scene nearly 100 years later—a little over 400 years before Christ is born—to preach on worshipping God, remembering God's love for them, and bringing the message of the coming Messiah.

 ## LESSON:

We have finally arrived at the last book of the Old Testament—Malachi, written just over 400 years before the birth of Christ. It's been about 1,500 years since God made His covenant with Abraham. At this point, the Jews have settled in Judah about 100 years after they began to return to the land God promised them in His covenant. Although Judah is still under Persian rule, the Jews are allowed to live in peace. Sometimes when things are too calm and peaceful, people tend to rely on themselves and take God for granted. Malachi reminds the Jews of God's love for them.

### (READ MALACHI 1:2)

Repeatedly, God has shown His love for His people even when His people turned their collective backs on Him. Malachi says when they remember God's love, they will have the right attitude toward God and His commands. Forgetting His love opens the door to placing their loyalty elsewhere, like false gods. Yet, while we read about the Israelites going back and forth in their loyalty to God, we also read about God's unchanging loyalty to them.

### (READ MALACHI 3:6-7)

The Old Testament reveals how the Israelites constantly seem to boomerang between God and false gods. They follow God's laws and

## BIBLE WORD OF THE DAY:

RETURN

Definition: Come back, as to a former place, position or state (Malachi 3:7).

"... 'Return to Me,' says the Lord of hosts, 'and I will return to you'..."
(Zechariah 1:3).

## BIBLE VERSES

Malachi 1:2
Malachi 3:6-7
Judges 3:7-8
Zechariah 10:6
Malachi 3:1

## BIG IDEA

(SCHOLAR & SCRIBE) God's plan of salvation in the New Testament has its roots in God's covenant with Abraham.

commands for a while, and then, for various reasons, worship the idols and man-made images of their neighbors in pagan nations. As we've studied, when the people become thoroughly immersed in the wickedness that accompanies idol-worship and refuse to return to the Lord and follow His ways, God disciplines them. Often He punishes them by allowing one of those pagan nations to rule over and oppress them. This happens more than once in Judges.

## BRING IT UP

**(SCHOLAR)** Why do you think it's important for Christians to study the Old Testament?

**(SCRIBE)** What has surprised you the most during our study of the Old Testament?

### (READ JUDGES 3:7-8)

After eight years, the children of Israel cry out to the Lord, who hears them and sends them Othniel, Caleb's younger brother, to deliver them. With the Spirit of the Lord upon him, Othniel goes to war and the Lord delivers Cushan-Rishathaim the king of Mesopotamia into his hands. For the next 40 years, Israel is at peace. But when Othniel dies, the children of Israel again do evil in the sight of the Lord.

It continues during the period of the Divided Kingdom, when Israel split into two different nations. Ruled over by 19 evil kings, Israel meets its punishment by God when Assyria invades and conquers the nation in 722 B.C. Almost 150 later, the southern kingdom of Judah, which has a few good but mostly evil kings, meets the same fate when the Babylonian Empire chips away at Judah for several years and eventually overtakes Jerusalem in 586 B.C. Before either of these kingdoms fall to pagan nations, God sends prophets to encourage their repentance and to warn them of the consequences if they fail to return to Him.

We read of the two captivities and two exoduses in the Old Testament: The captivity and exodus out of Egypt and the captivity and exodus out of Babylon. Both times, God shows His mercy and love for His people. Both times, God keeps His promises to them.

### (READ ZECHARIAH 10:6)

Another promise God makes—which He does throughout the Old Testament—is to send His Son as part of a new covenant to all people.

### (READ MALACHI 3:1)

The messenger who "will prepare the way" refers to John the Baptist (Mark 1:1-4), and the Messenger of the covenant is Jesus (Matthew 26:28). Jesus, also called the Christ, has many names. For example, in John 1:1-2, Jesus is the Word who has always been with God. It is through Jesus and this new covenant that all may receive God's mercy and love, the way the Israelites received God's mercy and love for over 1,500 years through His covenant with Abraham. This new covenant as fully revealed in the New Testament is God's plan of salvation.

---

 **BIBLE BASICS:**

1. What is the last book of the Old Testament? **Malachi**

2. When Malachi is written, how many years is it before the birth of Christ? **Just over 400 years**
3. When Malachi is written, how many years has it been since God's covenant with Abraham? **About 1,500 years**
4. Under what country's rule is Judah still? **Persia**
5. Of what does Malachi remind the Jews? **God's love**
6. Often, when God's people turn to false gods, how does He punish them? **By allowing pagan nations to rule over them**
7. Who is Caleb's younger brother that God raises up to deliver the people from the king of Mesopotamia? **Othniel**
8. When Othniel dies, what do the children of Israel resume doing? **Evil in the sight of the Lord**
9. Which nation is ruled solely by evil kings? **Israel**
10. What two countries hold the children of Israel captive? **Egypt and Babylon**
11. Who is the messenger who will prepare the way? **John the Baptist**
12. Who is the Messenger of the new covenant? **Jesus**

---

# BESIDE THE POINT:

**(SCHOLAR)** Peppered throughout the Old Testament are prophecies concerning Christ, written hundreds of years before He is born. The following verses of prophecies and their fulfillments allow the students to see for themselves how the Old Testament and the New Testament go hand in hand.

| Prophecy: Jesus will be… | Fulfillment |
| --- | --- |
| A descendant of Abraham (Genesis 12:3) | Matthew 1:1 |
| A descendant of Jacob (Numbers 24:17) | Matthew 1:2 |
| A descendant of Judah (Genesis 49:10) | Luke 3:33 |
| Heir of the throne of David (Isaiah 9:7) | Luke 1:32-33 |
| Crucified (Psalm 22:16) | John 19:18 |
| Pierced (Zechariah 12:10) | John 19:34 |
| Buried in Rich Man's Tomb (Isaiah 53:9) | John 19:38-42 |

**(SCRIBE)** As a quick review of prominent Old Testament events, put the following in chronological order.

- A. Nahum preaches to Ninevah
- B. Jericho falls
- C. God calls Moses to lead His people
- D. Joseph becomes governor in Egypt
- E. Malachi writes the last book of the Old Testament
- F. Delilah tricks Samson
- G. Jonah is tossed overboard
- H. Israel falls
- I. Isaac marries Rebekah
- J. Hannah prays for a son
- K. Solomon builds the temple
- L. God makes His covenant with Abraham
- M. Jacob gives a bowl of stew to Esau

N. Daniel is tossed into a lions' den
O. Zerubbabel returns with the first group of Jews
P. Judah falls
Q. Hezekiah gains 15 years of life
R. Haman hangs on the gallows
S. David kills Goliath
T. Elijah is taken up in a whirlwind

---

 ## BRING IT HOME:

**(SCHOLAR & SCRIBE)** With your parents and other family members, read Romans 15:4 and 1 Corinthians 10:6-11 about the importance of the Old Testament. What are some specific lessons we can learn from the Old Testament that we can apply in our study of the New Testament?

---

 ## BEYOND THE LESSON:

**(SCHOLAR)** Besides prophecies concerning Christ, the Old Testament contains many "foreshadowing" references to Him. An example is Exodus 12:43-46 that gives instructions to the people about the Passover meal. Read the passage. What does verse 46 foreshadow? (Hint—John 19:33, 36)

Answer: **Jesus' bones will not be broken as a result of His crucifixion**

**(SCRIBE)** In God's covenant with Abraham, God promises that the Christ will descend from him. Abraham has two sons, Ishmael (with Sarah's handmaid Hagar), and Isaac (with Sarah). Read Genesis 17:19 and Luke 3:34. Through which son does Christ descend?

Answer: **Isaac**

# FLASHCARDS
# THE 39 OLD TESTAMENT BOOKS

For best results, it is recommended that you photocopy these on cardstock (so the student cannot see the answers through the paper), cut them out, and then laminate them.

**GENESIS**

**EXODUS**

**LEVITICUS**

**NUMBERS**

**SUPPLEMENTAL MATERIAL**

# COUNTING PEOPLE   LEAVING EGYPT

# BEGINNINGS

# LAWS

**WRITTEN FOR OUR LEARNING**

| JOSHUA | DEUTERONOMY |
|---|---|
| RUTH | JUDGES |

SUPPLEMENTAL MATERIAL

**CONQUERING CANAAN**

**SECOND LAW**

**LOYALTY**

**EARLY LEADERS**

# 1 SAMUEL

# 2 SAMUEL

# 1 KINGS

# 2 KINGS

**SUPPLEMENTAL MATERIAL**

**KING DAVID**

**SAMUEL, SAUL, DAVID**

**DIVIDED KINGDOM**

**SOLOMON**

# 1 CHRONICLES

# 2 CHRONICLES

# EZRA

# NEHEMIAH

**SUPPLEMENTAL MATERIAL**

# KINGS OF JUDAH

# DAVID'S REIGN

# NEW WALLS

# NEW TEMPLE

**WRITTEN FOR OUR LEARNING**

| ESTHER | JOB |
| --- | --- |
| PSALMS | PROVERBS |

SUPPLEMENTAL MATERIAL

GOD ALLOWS SUFFERING

COURAGEOUS QUEEN

WISDOM OF SOLOMON

POETRY, SONGS OF DAVID

**WRITTEN FOR OUR LEARNING**

# SONG OF SOLOMON

# ECCLESIASTES

# JEREMIAH

# ISAIAH

**SUPPLEMENTAL MATERIAL**

LOVE POEM

MEANING OF LIFE

CRIES TO SAVE JUDAH

PROPHECIES ABOUT CHRIST

**WRITTEN FOR OUR LEARNING**

# LAMENTATIONS

# EZEKIEL

# DANIEL

# HOSEA

**SUPPLEMENTAL MATERIAL** 143

**VALLEY OF BONES**

**FALL OF JUDAH**

**UNFAITHFUL WIFE**

**LIONS' DEN**

AMOS

JOEL

JONAH

OBADIAH

**SUPPLEMENTAL MATERIAL**

# FARMER PROPHESIES

# LOCUSTS

# GOD'S GRACE RECEIVED

# PUNISHMENT FOR EDOM

NAHUM

MICAH

ZEPHANIAH

HABAKKUK

**SUPPLEMENTAL MATERIAL**

# GOD'S GRACE REJECTED

# DOOM THEN HOPE

# LAST CHANCE TO REPENT

# ASKING GOD, "WHY?"

ZECHARIAH

HAGGAI

MALACHI

SUPPLEMENTAL MATERIAL

# VISIONS FOR RETURNING EXILES

# FIXING GOD'S HOUSE

# PROPER WORSHIP

# FLASHCARDS
# 39 OLD TESTAMENT PERSONALITIES

ABRAHAM

SARAH

ISAAC

REBEKAH

**SUPPLEMENTAL MATERIAL**

**ABRAHAM'S WIFE**

**FATHER OF ALL NATIONS**

**ISAAC'S WIFE**

**ABRAHAM'S SON**

152 **WRITTEN FOR OUR LEARNING**

| JACOB (ISRAEL) | ESAU |
|---|---|
| LEAH | RACHEL |

SUPPLEMENTAL MATERIAL

**JACOB'S TWIN**

**FATHER OF 12 TRIBES**

**JACOB'S BELOVED WIFE**

**JACOB'S FIRST WIFE**

| JOSEPH | BENJAMIN |
| --- | --- |
| JUDAH | MOSES |

**JACOB'S YOUNGEST SON**

**SOLD INTO SLAVERY**

**HEBREW DELIVERER**

**JESUS' EARTHLY TRIBE**

**WRITTEN FOR OUR LEARNING**

| JOSHUA | AARON |

| RAHAB | CALEB |

MOSES' SUCCESSOR

MOSES' SPOKESMAN

SPIES' HELPER

BRAVE SPY

**WRITTEN FOR OUR LEARNING**

| GIDEON | EHUD |
|---|---|
| JOB | SAMSON |

**SUPPLEMENTAL MATERIAL**

**FLEECE-WATCHING JUDGE**

**LEFT-HANDED JUDGE**

**GOD-FEARING SUFFERER**

**LONG-HAIRED JUDGE**

| RUTH | HANNAH |
|---|---|
| SAMUEL | SAUL |

SUPPLEMENTAL MATERIAL

**PRAYERFUL MOTHER**

**LOYAL DAUGHTER-IN-LAW**

**RELUCTANT KING**

**JUDGE AND PROPHET**

UZZAH

DAVID

AHAB

SOLOMON

**SUPPLEMENTAL MATERIAL**

ARK-CATCHER

AFTER GOD'S HEART

WICKED KING

WISE TEMPLE-BUILDER

| MANASSEH | ELIJAH |
| --- | --- |
| ELISHA | JOASH |

**SUPPLEMENTAL MATERIAL**

**WHIRLWIND PROPHET**

**REPENTANT KING**

**BOY KING**

**ELIJAH'S MANTLE-CARRIER**

NAAMAN

JOSIAH

JEREMIAH

HEZEKIAH

**LEPER RIVER-DIPPER**

**LAW-RESTORER**

**SAD PROPHET**

**PROPHET WITH EXTENDED LIFE**

ESTHER

JONAH

DANIEL

**SUPPLEMENTAL MATERIAL**

**RUNAWAY PROPHET**

**INTERVENING QUEEN**

**LION-TAMER**

**WRITTEN FOR OUR LEARNING**

# WRITTEN FOR OUR LEARNING TIMELINE

| | |
|---|---|
| The Covenant | 2080 B.C. |
| Isaac and Rebekah | 2020 B.C. |
| Jacob and Esau | 1980 B.C. |
| Job | 1900 B.C.* |
| Joseph | 1910 B.C. |
| Moses | 1450 B.C. |
| Golden Calf | 1450 B.C. |
| Fall of Jericho | 1410 B.C. |
| Ehud | 1360 B.C. |
| Samson | 1150 B.C. |
| Hannah and Samuel | 1140 B.C. |
| Saul and David | 1047 B.C. |
| Uzzah | 1000 B.C. |
| Solomon | 940 B.C. |
| Divided Kingdom | 930 B.C. |
| Elijah | 860 B.C. |
| Ahab | 855 B.C. |
| Elisha | 850 B.C. |
| Naaman | 845 B.C. |
| Joel | 835 B.C. |
| Athaliah and Joash | 835 B.C. |
| Jonah | 780 B.C. |
| Isaiah | 725 B.C. |
| Israel Falls | 722 B.C. |
| Hezekiah | 700 B.C. |
| Josiah | 640 B.C. |
| Habakkuk | 620 B.C. |
| Nahum | 615 B.C. |
| Jeremiah | 600 B.C. |
| Ezekiel | 590 B.C. |
| Judah Falls | 586 B.C. |
| Daniel | 540 B.C. |
| Haggai | 520 B.C. |
| Zechariah | 520 B.C. |
| Esther | 475 B.C. |
| Ezra | 460 B.C. |
| Nehemiah | 460 B.C. |
| Malachi | 430 B.C. |

*It is not known exactly when Job lived; however, the book of Job offers clues that suggest Job lived after the Flood (2350 B.C.) and before the birth of Moses (1530 B.C.), and probably around the beginning of the Patriarch Age.

# MAJOR EVENTS REFERENCE TIMELINE
(Years are Estimates)

| | |
|---|---|
| Creation Adam and Eve | 4000 B.C. |
| The Flood | 2350 B.C. |
| Tower of Babel | 2250 B.C. |
| The Covenant | 2080 B.C. |
| 12 Tribes of Israel | 1940 B.C. |
| Israelites' Captivity in Egypt | 1890 B.C. |
| Israelites' Exodus from Egypt | 1450 B.C. |
| End of Wandering in the Wilderness | 1410 B.C. |
| Canaan Conquest | 1400 B.C. |
| Judges Rule | 1400 B.C. |
| Kings Rule | 1047 B.C. |
| Divided Kingdom | 930 B.C. |
| Assyrian Destruction of Israel | 722 B.C. |
| Fall of Jerusalem/Babylonian Captivity | 586 B.C. |
| Persian Conquest of Babylonian Empire | 539 B.C. |
| Jews Return Home | 536 B.C. |
| Temple Rebuilt | 515 B.C. |
| Malachi Written | 430 B.C. |

**SUPPLEMENTAL MATERIAL**

www.ingramcontent.com/pod-product-compliance
Lightning Source LLC
Chambersburg PA
CBHW051407070526
44584CB00023B/3332